The Internet

ISSUES
(formerly Issues for the Nineties)

Volume 31

Editor

Craig Donnellan

Independence

First published by Independence
PO Box 295
Cambridge CB1 3XP
England

© Craig Donnellan 1999

British Library Cataloguing in Publication Data
The Internet – (Issues Series)
I. Donnellan, Craig II. Series
004.6'78

ISBN 1 86168 103 8

Printed in Great Britain
The Burlington Press
Cambridge

Typeset by
Claire Boyd

Cover
The illustration on the front cover is by
Pumpkin House.

CONTENTS

Chapter One: The Internet in Schools

Chapter Two: The Internet in the Home

Introduction

The Internet is the thirty-first volume in the **Issues** series. The aim of this series is to offer up-to-date information about important issues in our world.

The Internet looks at the benefits and dangers of the internet, both in schools and in the home.

The information comes from a wide variety of sources and includes:
Government reports and statistics
Newspaper reports and features
Magazine articles and surveys
Literature from lobby groups
and charitable organisations.

It is hoped that, as you read about the many aspects of the issues explored in this book, you will critically evaluate the information presented. It is important that you decide whether you are being presented with facts or opinions. Does the writer give a biased or an unbiased report? If an opinion is being expressed, do you agree with the writer?

The Internet offers a useful starting-point for those who need convenient access to information about the many issues involved. However, it is only a starting-point. At the back of the book is a list of organisations which you may want to contact for further information.

*****

Top marks: the web shows the way

**The Internet can take the headache out of revision.
Debbie Davies explains how to make the most of it**

The enormous increase in the number of homes with computers and Internet access means pupils taking GCSE this year have a new medium to help with revision.

One of the most popular Web sites is GCSE Answers (www.gcse.com), which covers English and maths and has been run for the past two years by a group of teachers.

'We receive about 100 enquiries a week,' says Philip Adams, the co-ordinator. 'About two-thirds ask for help with coursework assignments. Our algebra tutorials are particularly popular.'

The maths tutorials, which include trigonometry and graphs, are divided into 'easy starts', for pupils aiming for a grade C, and 'heavy duty stuff' for those hoping for an A or A*. Questions are followed by a step-by-step guide to the answers, a useful way to revise.

The English department does not try to cover all the set literature texts but contains useful sections on language and poetry. There is also advice on coursework folders, a list of the most commonly misspelt words, model answers and test-yourself tutorials.

There is no charge for using the Web site, apart from the cost of the local phone call to connect to the Internet.

Another popular Web site offering on-line tutorials is GCSE Bitesize (www.bbc.co.uk/education/revision). Published by BBC Education and based on manageable chunks of revision, it is the only guide to use television, books (£4.99 each) and the Internet; for maths there is also a new CD-Rom (£19.99).

An interactive element enables pupils to test themselves and receive feedback on their performance. They can e-mail teachers with their problems and swap messages with others.

Pupils at Monkseaton High School in Whitley Bay, Tyne and Wear, who used the Web site last year had their performance evaluated by Durham University. Their results were between half and a full grade higher than expected.

'Bitesize appealed to our students because it included television programmes and the Internet,' says Dr Paul Kelley, the headteacher.

The biggest effect was on French, where results rose by a full grade. History saw no improvement because the revision course did not follow the syllabus Monkseaton was using.

Good as they are, neither of these Web sites makes full use of the Internet's ability to bring people together. To see the Internet at its most interactive, try Virtual School (www.virtualschool.co.uk), a site that offers one-to-one revision lessons using audio conferencing. A one-hour tutorial costs £10; e-mail assignments cost £4, which includes the marking of a pupil's work.

Taking part is easy. Virtual School uses a software program called NetMeeting, which comes as a part of Internet Explorer, Microsoft's browser program. It can also be downloaded from Microsoft's Web site at no charge. Teacher and pupil talk as if on the phone. Both can see an exercise on the screen, and the mouse pointer becomes a pen for underlining or highlighting text. Written contributions appear on screen as they are typed.

Pupils like Virtual School because it makes revision remarkably easy.

'With a book, you can start revising and then a friend phones or you might just decide not to do anything,' says Henry Procter, 15, who has used Virtual School for his English revision.

'With Virtual School, you have to concentrate and interact with the teacher like you do in class, but it's not embarrassing when you don't know the answer because the teacher can't see you.'

For the less disciplined pupil, Virtual School accomplishes a lot in one hour.

Perhaps companies that are so keen to connect us all to the Internet should think more about supporting its educational potential with their own cyber schools as the exams approach. Most Internet service providers stage live discussions with people in the news in which anyone can take part. In the run-up to a

GCSE exam, pupils might welcome a chat with a teacher.

A Web site from which you could download past exam papers would be useful, too. Unfortunately, the GCSE boards have been reluctant to put the papers on the Internet, fearing a loss of income. However, under competitive pressure from the growing number of Web sites run by teachers, this may be about to change. As a trial, the Northern Examinations Assessment Board has decided to publish past papers, together with examiners' marking schemes and

comments in a limited number of subjects. These should be posted up on its Web site (www.neab.ac.uk) soon.

For general information on Bitesize, call 0181 746 1111. Books and CD-Roms are available from all good bookshops or call 01937 541001. Other resources written by teachers for GCSE that are worth a visit:

Maths: www.maths-help.co.uk
Science: www.purchon.co.uk/science/index.html; www.wbateman.demon.co.uk
History: www.historychannel.co.uk; www.bbc.co.uk/education/modern/mainmenu
Geography: www.pavilion.co.uk/dwakefield
Art: www.schoolart.co.uk
Music: big.jessie.com
Drama: www.killay.demon.co.uk/index.htm

• First published in *The Daily Telegraph*, March 1999.   ©*Debbie Davies*

Getting on the Net

What do schools need to think about?

To get on the Net you need not just a computer, telephone and a modem; you also need to be very clear about why you want to go on-line. We list some of the things schools need to consider.

Things that schools should think about before going on-line

- Why is the school investing in Internet access?
- What kind of connection should the school invest in?
- Where should access points be?
- When and for how long should there be on-line access?
- Who will be able to access the Internet – teachers, pupils, other staff, governors?
- Who will be responsible for managing the Internet?

Where should e-mail/Internet computer be sited?

It is best to identify the group who will need most access time and site

the relevant computer to suit them.

Staffroom – there is a strong argument for siting the computer in the staffroom, especially in schools where teachers have not all used the Internet already.

Library – if placed in the library it establishes the computer as a new and significant reference resource. Its use and development will be dependent on either the librarian/library postholder or on a commitment from members of staff.

School office – in a primary school it may be useful to have the on-line computer near the school office so that there is some background supervision or adult help near at hand should the technology quaver.

What is the school's Internet policy?

The issues of Internet safety, security, use, access, management, etc. should be discussed with staff and pupils in the school. Obviously the level of

the discussion will vary according to the age of the pupils.

Your school should devise a school policy which takes into account all those issues and which can be agreed by parents and pupils. Everyone should be clear about what is acceptable and what is not acceptable in your school as regards the Internet, e-mail, discussion groups and chat areas.

How can you avoid children seeing unsuitable material?

You need to install filtering software on your computer or network (we have listed a few examples below). The administrator will have a password and will control the options chosen to filter out content according to the rules set in the software. None of them will completely solve the problem of unsuitable material being displayed, but they can certainly help.

Cyper Patrol has many options to restrict access according to a wide range of criteria, including time spent on-line and specific sites or areas of the Internet. Net Nanny uses lists of forbidden sites, words or phrases. Net Shepherd is a rating and filtering tool.

What do schools need to get on-line?

To get connected to the Internet you will need a computer, a telephone line, modem and Internet Service Provider (ISP).

What is a modem?

A modem is a small box connected to a computer, or installed inside it, that converts the digital signals from your computer into a form to be sent down the telephone line. The faster the modem the less time you will spend on the phone sending data like e-mail. Modem speeds are measured in bits per second (bps) and can vary from 14 bps to 56 bps.

The faster modems are usually more expensive; prices vary from £50 to £200, plus line costs, plus call charges.

What is an Internet service provider (ISP)?

An Internet service provider is a company which sells you a connection to the Internet, which you can reach with a local phone call from your computer. Having an account with a service provider gives you access to the World Wide Web, e-mail and many other services.

Some questions to ask providers before you sign up:

- How long has the company been established?
- Does the company support the type of computer you use, e.g. PC, Apple, Acorn. (Some companies do not support all types.)
- Can you access the Internet for the price of a local call?
- What hours are their support phone lines open? Are they open at weekends?
- What is the start-up cost?
- What is the monthly fee and how can you pay?
- Do they offer full access, e.g. Point of Presence (POP) connection? (To use the World Wide Web you need a full connection to the Internet.)

Is virus protection needed for the Internet?

It is essential to install virus protection software on any computer or network which will be used for downloading anything from the Internet.

E-mail can also carry a virus in an attached file. Two well-known programs are Doctor Solomon and McAfee.

What if you find illegal material on the Internet?

The Internet Watch Foundation is an organisation set up to report on illegal material on the Internet. Their phone number is 01223 236077. Remember, you should report any illegal material you find to your service provider and to the police. Material that is illegal in print in this country is also illegal when downloaded from the Internet.

Computers can do a better job than teachers, says Blair aide

By Steve Doughty

Most teachers should be replaced by computers, a senior associate of Tony Blair declared yesterday. MP Margaret Hodge, leader of the influential Commons Education Select Committee, claimed many were stuck in a '1970s time warp'.

She said too few 'good-quality people' wanted to be teachers, and that in future much of their work should be done by 'information technology and learning through the Internet'.

Mrs Hodges, MP for Barking and a figure close to the heart of New Labour, said pupils should be helped by an 'elite force' of highly-trained and motivated teachers. But supervision of classes, marking and preparation of lessons should be carried out mainly by 'less well-trained assistants'.

The MP, former Left-wing leader of Islington Council in North London, has already upset teaching unions with a call for long school holidays to be abolished in favour of year-round education. Her latest broadside in the *New Statesman* magazine is certain to create fresh unease.

Mrs Hodge said that students on undergraduate training courses usually held poor A-level grades, with the average 'no better than two Ds and an E'.

Teaching jobs were difficult to fill because of the poor quality of applicants. 'Sadly the teachers themselves – or at least their representatives – are not much help in improving the profession's image,' she went on. 'Much of it remains stuck in a 1970s time warp.

'When the public think of teachers, they think of militant unions, resistance to change and long holidays. The image does the majority of hard-working, dedicated teachers no justice.'

Mrs Hodge said below-standard applicants should not be given teaching jobs 'purely to make up the numbers'. Information technology was about to revolutionise schools. 'In a few years I believe some classes will not be led by a fully-trained teacher,' she added.

Doug McAvoy, general secretary of the National Union of Teachers, said: 'Successive governments have failed to reward teachers and to ensure that conditions of service are good.

'They must bear the responsibility for teaching not being the first choice of career for young people.'

Nigel de Gruchy, general secretary of the National Association of Schoolmasters/Union of Women Teachers, said: 'Mrs Hodge is determined to make her name.

'But all she is achieving is to upset or demean everyone else.'

You can't beat chalk and talk

Teachers are increasingly sceptical about the benefits of computers in classrooms. John Clare can see why

The Government is spending £1 billion over the next four years introducing information and communication technology (ICT) into schools. Yet, as Charles Clarke, the junior education minister, admitted last week, there is still scarcely any evidence that computers in the classroom raise educational standards.

After 10 years of investment and research, all we know for certain is that one or two computer programs, when skilfully managed, are a useful way of teaching basic literacy and numeracy. The rest amounts to little more than substituting CD-Roms for teaching and books and, in the case of the Internet, distracting children from learning under the guise of 'doing research'.

That may explain why, according to a recent but unpublicised study by the Department for Education and Employment, the proportion of teachers who think ICT has anything to contribute to teaching has declined sharply over the past two years.

Of course, it is important that school-leavers should be familiar with the technology they will encounter at work – though nearly everyone now using it learnt their skills on the job – but is that really an argument for computers to pervade the curriculum, as the Government demands, or for such a massive diversion of educational resources?

The only possible justification would be a belief that most teachers are not up to the job and need to be computer-assisted if standards are to rise. Is that really what the Government thinks?

Such questions were prompted by last week's Educational Technology Show at Olympia, west London, billed as the biggest of its kind in the world – not surprising when there is so much cash washing about.

Indeed, touring the 360 stands, it was difficult to shake off the feeling that further resistance was futile; that,

given the strength of the Government's commitment, the rising tide of technology had become unstoppable. What, after all, is the point of objecting that most CD-Roms are merely cumbersome, expensive books with spurious bells and whistles when there seems to be no money for books but any amount for CD-Roms?

So what do the latest developments in educational technology have to offer? By far the most interesting on show last week was Future School, a system for teaching national curriculum English and maths to children aged five to 18. Ironically, it represents a full-blooded return to old fashioned chalk and talk.

Teachers are the last bulwark against the tide of mindless technology now lapping at the school gates. They deserve all the support sceptical parents can offer

---

Each pupil sits at a screen wearing headphones and watches a video of a teacher who stands in front of a blackboard and teaches. One advantage is that anyone who has not understood something can simply stop the lesson, rewind and listen again. Another is that bright

children are free to forge ahead while the class teacher concentrates on those who are struggling.

Developed in Australia during the mid-Eighties as a set of home-based learning materials. Future School offers no gimmicks, cartoons or sound effects – just lucid instruction. It calls itself 'the dawning of the new era in teaching and learning' – if only it were so.

At its worst, software uses the power of ICT to overwhelm the subject matter and become an end in itself. One example on show was Auralog, 'the first language learning method entirely based on speech recognition technology'. It requires students to keep pronouncing words until their 'voice print' matches that of a native speaker, an elaborate way of replacing the sound the ear can hear with a graph for the eye to read – helpful for deaf people but otherwise a useless distraction.

Even worse were CD-Roms such as the *Basics in a Nutshell* series, produced by Re-Animate (at £49.99 each). Purporting to teach grammar and punctuation, they present the information in the form of a mind-numbing television show, which is hosted by a pair of frenetic cartoon characters.

So complete is the contrast between format and material that comprehension drops to zero. Far from 'bringing learning to life' – this

year's most popular sales slogan – the technology actually undermines the user's concentration and destroys understanding.

At its best – in, for example, *Multimedia Chemistry School*, sponsored by the Nuffield Foundation – a CD-Rom system uses animated graphics, text and video clips to illuminate the complex, enabling pupils to grasp what is otherwise hard for teachers to explain.

Examples of that, though, are rare. Far more common are elaborate packages, such as Kingscourt's *Inside Stories* ('making multimedia a vital part of literacy education'), that aim to teach children what every parent would rather a real teacher taught them.

Teachers, it seems, increasingly feel the same. Castigated by the Government and the ICT industry for their lack of enthusiasm and expertise, they are the last bulwark against the tide of mindless technology now lapping at the school gates. They deserve all the support sceptical parents can offer.

A computer is only as good as its master

Computers have redefined the culture of our age, but they will always take second place to the ability of the human brain

Book Review by
Rachelle Thackray

Everyone is familiar with the term 'digital age'. Even if few of us know precisely what it means, we all associate it with the oft-breaking and ever-higher waves of modern technology from which, we enthusiastically imagine, will emerge a brave new future.

At the height of this age, technology will produce fruits of which we have only dreamt. The mundane decisions of life, together with tedious chores such as manually turning on the television set, sending a letter through the post or heaving home a bag of groceries, will long since have been taken out of our hands by computers that anticipate our every need.

Yet the children of the Seventies who fantasised in their school competitions about 'What It Will Be Like in the Year 2000' are still waiting for the advent of personalised travel capsules and know-it-all robots which once seemed sure to follow in the footsteps of R2D2. Are children of the Nineties just as misguided in believing that such inventions of the mind are likely to become reality?

Charles Jonscher, who trained in electrical sciences at Cambridge and now runs an investment firm, is refreshingly sceptical of the assumption that computers, in their various incarnations, hold the keys to richer life in the 21st century. In his new book, he insists instead that their role will always be secondary to the human beings who designed and created them.

A more interesting issue is the way that computers have helped to redefine the identity and the culture of the age. He writes: 'We certainly do not need to buy into a new philosophy of life, a sort of cyber-ontology in which the meaning of existence has been solved by deciding that we are computers.' And he adds: 'The computer revolution is a subplot in a bigger revolution: the explosion of human knowledge in all its forms.'

With his argument that humans, rather than technology, will always have the upper hand, Jonscher begins a fascinating unravelling of where the 'digital age' has sprung from, with all its limitations and possibilities. While lauding the technology which could now record every moment of a human life by means of a tiny bit of silicon implanted in the brain – the apocryphal 'soul-catcher' chip – he points out that the human brain itself has 20 billion neurons, capable of 100 trillion connections (a single neuron can connect with 80,000 others). 'Comparing a neuron to a single silicon switch?' he asks. 'The intelligence of a single-cell organism less evolved than a neuron, such as a paramecium, is such that it can navigate towards food and negotiate obstacles, recognise danger and retreat from it. How does your PC compare?'

There are some illuminating definitions here: knowledge, notes the author, is a state of being, while information, which comes from the root 'to inform', is transitive, and to be used fleetingly.

Jonscher also levels the stun-gun at some sacred cows, such as the idea that artificial intelligence could evolve to take over the world in the manner described in Philip Kerr's thriller novel *Gridiron*. And after a delve through the scientific theories lying behind the evolution of IT, he goes on to trace its development, with its impact on and creation of multimedia and the Internet, economic progress and the 'productivity paradox', and the technologies of tomorrow.

For anyone who has ever asked what the IT revolution is all about, and how it will affect them, this readable and authoritative account, with its occasional dashes of dry humour, will fill some of the gaps.

Best of all, Jonscher never loses sight of his own argument. As he succinctly sums up: 'We must not mistake gigabytes for wisdom.'
Wired Life: Who are we in the digital age? By Charles Jonscher, Bantam, £14.99.
• First published in *The Independent*, March, 1999.   © *Rachelle Thackray*

Computers with no common sense

By Michio Kaku

With computer power doubling every 18 months (Moore's Law), some experts in artificial intelligence are now bragging that by 2050, robots will surpass the intelligence of humans. They boast that their creations may one day treat us like pets, too feeble and stupid to take care of ourselves. Robots will inherit the earth, and perhaps place us in zoos. The scientists at Carnegie-Mellon Institute, with the largest robotics laboratory in the world, even claim that we are creating our own Darwinian successors, that it's our evolutionary duty to prepare the way for super-intelligent robots, as if it's a law of nature.

But no so fast! The rosy claims of these mathematicians are not without some merit, but they have been made before, with laughable results. As a physicist, I must note that there are a few tiny roadblocks in their predictions, such as the laws of physics.

It is true that Moore's Law has successfully predicted the staggering growth of computers for the past 50 years. This means that every Christmas, our computer gadgets are almost twice as powerful as the previous year's. It's also true that our brains, even when daydreaming, compute at more than 500 trillion bytes per second. By Moore's Law, our chips should hit about 500 trillion bytes per second by 2050.

But there are also tremendous roadblocks. For instance, Moore's Law will collapse way before 2050. In fact, by 2020, transistors will become so small, they will approach the size of DNA coils. Unfortunately, silicon is not structurally stable at such tiny distances. Silicon Valley may become a Rust Belt by 2020 – the Age of Silicon will end, causing chaos in the computer business.

After 2020, physicists will have to replace silicon with very speculative designs, such as computers which compute on laser beams, DNA molecules, protein molecules, or single electrons. There's also the ultimate computer, the 'quantum computer', which is so advanced that no prototypes even exist. These are all highly risky designs, so all bets are off after 2020.

Furthermore, scientists have not solved the problem of 'common sense'. Computers don't know the things that even children know. Computers don't know that water is wet, that animals don't like pain, that mothers are older than their children, that twins age at the same rate, and that when you die you don't come back the next day. How do we know these commonsense things? By experience. But that's precisely what computers don't have. Worse, mathematicians believe that several hundred million statements of common sense are required before a robot can reason like a child. This staggering amount of common sense has effectively stopped progress in artificial intelligence for the past 20 years.

Finally, computers don't see very well. One of the most advanced robots is the Mars Rover, currently on the planet Mars. Although the Mars Rover captured the imagination of millions of people around the world, it has the intelligence of a retarded cockroach. Even a cockroach knows how to flee when spotted on your kitchen table. If a Martian were to swat the Mars Rover with its tentacle, the Rover would take several hours to realise that the tentacle was not a rock!

This is not to say that we won't have computer marvels by 2050. By then, chips will cost a fraction of a penny, the cost of bubble gum wrappers. We will have computers in our watches, clothes, jewellery, furniture, walls, appliances, and perhaps inside our bodies. And we will talk to them in English, albeit a highly stylised and simple English. But don't expect to have robot butlers or maids by 2050.

In other words, don't worry; the mathematicians are wrong. Humanity is not doomed to live in a cage after 2050. (Unless, of course, we physicists can invent the quantum computer . . .)

Michio Kaku is the author of *Visions* (Oxford University Press, £8.99)

• First published in *The Independent*, March, 1999.   © *Michio Kaku*

New face of homework

Victoria Greaves goes back to school to learn that those IT winds of change are reaching gale force

I always knew I would feel old one day and find myself mumbling 'Things were never like this in my day.' I was dismayed when I visited a school last week and heard myself say it . . . just eight years after burning my A-level books.

The wind of technological change is blowing a gale and Duston Upper School in Northampton has managed in just two years to transform a criticised and under-provided IT department into an impressive network of desktop PCs, portable computers, scanners and laser printers.

David Anstead, the deputy head, is the driving force behind this IT revolution.

'An Ofsted report was quite critical of our IT provision and our IT work was slightly below curriculum standards,' he recalls. 'We had to devise a strategy which would allow us to maximise use of our existing facilities while expanding within what we could afford.'

A fibre optic network was already fitted around the school but there wasn't much attached to it. Three computers in the resource centre – in my day we used to call it the library – were in almost constant use, but timetable restrictions meant that the computer rooms were in use for less than 50 per cent of their available time.

'We couldn't afford large suites of PCs in each faculty area, so we looked at the problem from the other way round and rather than lead the students to technology we decided to take technology to the students,' explains Anstead.

Much detailed research later, Duston invested in a pool of 40 Apple eMate 300s portable computers for around £399 each. They also part-funded and used local sponsorship for the necessary £100,000 to buy 60 new PCs, install a server, and provide scanners and laser printers for each computer suite. The Government provided £3,800 for Internet connection costs.

A full-time technician is responsible for maintaining and logging the use of eMates, which were specially designed for school use. Any pupil can book one out for a lesson or to take home for doing homework. Their reputation for being robust will be tested this month when they are taken on their first big science field trip.

'They've proved they can stand the occasional drop but we'll have to see how they cope out in the field,' says Anstead.

Each pupil has a personal logon and user area on the network. Work done on the eMate is downloaded on to the network and can be developed into a larger project using Windows NT 4.0 on a desktop PC. The eMate's touch-sensitive screen means pupils can download graphics they draw and incorporate them with text, tables or scanned images.

'I prefer to do homework if I've got the eMate at home and I probably spend longer on it than when I'm just using textbooks'

This is the school's first year of using the eMates properly and Anstead admits they are still working out baselines of capability and usefulness. Laurence Ryan and Victoria Wrigg, who are both in Year 10, are keen to get more use out of the eMates than at present.

'I'd like to use them more often in class but sometimes the teacher doesn't want us to because she doesn't really know how to use them,' says Ryan.

Wrigg agrees that most pupils are keen to use the eMates more. 'I prefer to do homework if I've got the eMate at home and I probably spend longer on it than when I'm just using textbooks,' she says.

The problem that children tend to take to computers more naturally than adults is next on Anstead's list of priorities. 'Most of the computer use is driven by students,' he admits. 'There's pressure from them to use the computers more and we are training the teachers so we can do that.'

The pupils are clearly chomping at the bit. While walking round the resource centre one of them pounces on Anstead. 'Have you got that Internet connection sorted out yet sir?' he demands. Anstead assures him that he's getting it sorted.

© *Telegraph Group Limited, London 1998*

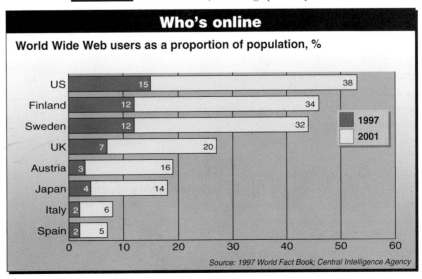

Who's online

World Wide Web users as a proportion of population, %

Country	1997	2001
US	15	38
Finland	12	34
Sweden	12	32
UK	7	20
Austria	3	16
Japan	4	14
Italy	2	6
Spain	2	5

Source: 1997 World Fact Book; Central Intelligence Agency

Parents get on-line for class check

By Tony Halpin

Parents will soon be able to find out what their children are studying at school under plans to put the new national curriculum on the internet.

The idea is that they will be able to see what is in every subject of the curriculum at each point in their children's education, learn more about what they are studying, and gain tips on ways to help them get more out of their lessons.

Advice on helping with homework and information on things such as home-school contracts would also be available, so that parents can get a better idea of what to expect from the teachers – and what they are expected to do in return. And all at the click of a mouse on a home computer.

Education Secretary David Blunkett sees the web site, announced as part of a wide-ranging review of the national curriculum, as another way of extending 'parent power' in schools. The more parents know, the more involved they will become in helping teachers to ensure their children succeed.

As researchers and teachers' unions never tire of pointing out, children spend more time out of school each day than in and what they do at home has as much impact on their educational achievement as what happens in the classroom.

The Department for Education and Employment plans to launch an experimental web site later this year and to have a fully-fledged version by September 2000, when the new curriculum will be introduced.

This will include suggestions for enriching pupils' learning, for instance, by pointing out museum exhibitions taking place locally that could add to their understanding of particular subjects being studied in history or art.

And there will be lists of suggested books that parents may want to choose from to read with their children at home.

Schools Minister Charles Clarke believes the website will allow parents to become more involved generally in their children's education by helping them to understand what schools are aiming to achieve in every subject.

It will also link to the growing number of 'home pages' designed by individual schools which he hopes will also grow into useful ways of keeping parents informed about their children's progress.

'We believe 95 per cent of parents want to help their children learn,' says Mr Clarke. 'Our job is to explain to parents what the national curriculum is and what their children are being asked to do, and indicate ways forward to help their children.'

Pupils in peril on the Internet

Teachers' fear over pornography via the classroom computer

By Tony Halpin, Education Correspondent

The power of the Internet to corrupt as well as educate was spelled out yesterday at a teachers' conference.

Pornographic images, racist propaganda and violent material could easily be accessed by children, even by accident, as schools are linked up.

Paedophile gangs have already targeted schools by using e-mail addresses to try to entice pupils into contacting them. The dangers were stressed as members of the Association of Teachers and Lecturers called for government action against obscene and inflammatory material.

They fear parents could accuse teachers of corrupting youngsters if pupils download offensive material in the classroom. Teachers believe they could even be prosecuted.

Michael Moore, head of information technology at Little Hulton community school near Bolton, said sixth formers at one comprehensive had already been sent messages to their personal e-mail addresses from a paedophile ring in Sheffield,

'They were inviting the students to take part in e-mailing with these paedophiles. Luckily the students reported it very quickly and the school put a stop to it,' he said.

Another teacher said he came across appalling Internet sites even though his school's computer system is protected by a 'nanny' program intended to block access to unsuitable material. Andy Garner, of Chantry High School in Ipswich, said he checked what might be available to 12-year-olds doing a project a project on the slave trade. The computer's Internet search came up with 'slave farm'. This stated there were 'pictures depicting men or women bound and being beaten, spanked or whipped'.

Mr Garner told the conference in Bournemouth that he easily accessed other offensive material even though it was a 'nannied site'.

A search for material on the Ku Klux Klan for fifth-form history students brought him to the Klan's own 'home page' which declared that mixed-race children were 'something ungodly'. Another site showed a photograph of a group of white girls beating up a black pupil.

The Government wants all 24,000 schools to have access to the Internet by 2000, with a personal e-mail address for every pupil. Teachers agreed that it offered massive educational potential, with access for all children to world-class libraries, art galleries, and international experts. But they said the Government had to insist on high quality 'firewall' programmes designed to filter out obscene material. Even so, delegates admitted there was little schools could do to ban pornography completely. Gloucestershire teacher Sue Gaynord said: 'The firewall packages may be adult proof. Children do get round them.'

Education Secretary David

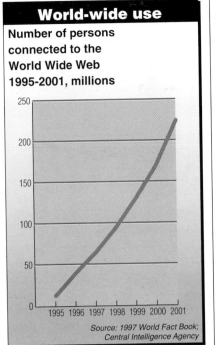

World-wide use

Number of persons connected to the World Wide Web 1995-2001, millions

Source: 1997 World Fact Book; Central Intelligence Agency

Blunkett said in a statement that he was determined to stamp out access to pornography so that pupils gained the full benefits of the Internet. He said it was vital that schools and education authorities had clear policies for protecting pupils.

One delegate told the conference that teachers should be educating pupils not to seek out such material rather than trying to ban it.

Terry Gallagher, from Nottinghamshire, said: 'We deal with sexism, racism and violence in schools. We should help them to make informed value judgements for themselves.'

Teacher Jakki Ellis, from south London, said parents had to play their part. 'We will do our best to protect their child from unsuitable material,' she said. 'But if their child chooses to circumvent our protections, the parents also have to ask themselves why. Their own moral guidance has failed.'

A number of programs have been developed by companies in an attempt to block access to unsuitable material. Some operate by barring 'sites' containing particular words.

Others rely on Internet surfers to alert them to the computer 'address' of offensive sites which are then placed on a blacklist. Schools can also link up to a closed 'intranet' service on which only carefully-vetted selection of sites are available. But this limits the effectiveness of the Internet as an educational tool.

© The Daily Mail
April, 1999

Community action to plug growing gap

Jack Schofield asks what is being done to meet the needs of pupils without home PCs

We can let technology be a negative force that furthers division, or we can use it to connect all Americans together and give them the same shot at success.'

There are no prizes for guessing who said that: US vice-president Al Gore. But change the nationality of the citizens referred to, and it could have been Tony Blair or, indeed, any ambitious politician from any of the industrialised nations.

Almost everyone agrees that exploiting ICT (information and communications technology) is the key to national and, increasingly, to corporate and even personal success. But if that's true, the uneven availability of ICT presents a social challenge. We are running the risk of creating classes of 'haves' and 'have nots': the information-rich and the information-poor.

The challenge for government and those publicly entrusted with the dissemination of knowledge – local education authorities, teachers, librarians and so on – is to do something about it.

The reasonably well-off parents can be left largely to their own devices. Prices have fallen so far that owning and running a home PC now costs about £5 a week, which is less than many families spend on alcohol, tobacco or even coffee. And with Dixons' FreeServe and Tesco's similar on-line service, families can now use the Internet for the cost of a local phone call: 1.5 pence a minute in the evenings and 1p a minute at weekends (plus VAT). However, even if parents buy computers for educational purposes, they may still be used mainly for playing games.

The less well-off certainly need help, and Becta (the British Educational Communications and Technology Agency), the Government's 'lead agency' for ICT and education is keen to explore ways to provide it. At this week's Education Show at the NEC in Birmingham, Becta will formally launch its Inclusion Projects Fund, which in its first year will pump £100,000 into 'stimulating the extension of ICT use beyond school and into the community'.

Chris Stevens, manager of special needs and inclusion at Becta, says: 'We aim to draw in communities – they may be isolated, rural, under-resourced, inner-city – who might otherwise be excluded from access to ICT. They will form working educational and vocational partner-ships that will be sustainable beyond Becta's involvement and will be replicable by others in similar situations. This is obviously not about solving the inclusion issue, but will be an exciting way to test and support good ideas for the future.'

However, there seem to be as many independent projects already under way as there are those managed by local education authorities. Some are sponsored by ICT suppliers such as Microsoft and IBM, some are com-mercial operations, such as Future-kids, and some depend on volunteers, such as Parent Teacher Associations. The simplest format is the 'homework club', which allows kids to use school computers after school.

But projects extend all the way to custom-built study centres, like the one Charlton Athletic FC has opened at its ground under the Playing For Success scheme whereby football clubs work with schools and education authorities, with state support.

The problem now is that many children have moved beyond com-puter literacy, which can be taught in a few hours a week, to using computers as tools. Some of them take notes on Psion and Windows CE-based hand-held computers, upload them to their home PCs, add supporting information from multi-media encylopaedias like Microsoft's Encarta, and print their resulting homework in high-resolution colour. Children who do not have more or less continuous access to the same equipment cannot easily produce the same results, no matter how talented they may be. It's hard not to agree with our friend Al Gore, who says:

'Access to the basic tools of the information age is no longer a luxury for our children. It is a necessity.' So why not give them all their own notebook computers, instead of boring old textbooks? Last summer, Dr Jack Christie, the chairman of the Texas State Board of Education, proposed exactly that, to local acclaim. (Well, Texas is the home of two of the world's three biggest PC manufacturers, Compaq and Dell.)

The obvious problem with this approach is covering the cost of the notebook PCs. In the UK, Microsoft joined up with hardware suppliers Acer, FujitsuICL and Hewlett-Packard to provide machines for its Anytime Anywhere Learning (AAL) project at huge discounts, but schools will still need help from PTAs, LEAs, and other sources to fund their purchases. Still, as Sawtry Com-munity College in Cambridgeshire has shown, portables can be treated as a bookable resource, and they could be rented out by the term, week or hour. If it's unrealistic for every child to have access to a computer all the time, there ought to be enough for the 'have nots' to share around.

Fair Share 1: Cincinnati

When impoverished US parents are given free on-line access to their children's teachers, miracles start to happen

IBM is running several five-year projects in the US in poorer school districts as part of its Reinventing Education programme, which in-volves applying the same sort of analysis techniques, software development and IT infrastructure to communities as it would to businesses. Last year it announced a $1 million investment in Ireland.

In Cincinnati, the school system is trying to move from traditional 'seat time' to performance-based schooling, with year-round opening and pay-for-performance plans that link teachers' salaries to student performance.

Robin Willner, director of corporate social policy at IBM, says: 'What we're trying to do in Cincinnati is break out of the rigid structure of 45 minutes for every subject every day, and allow students to proceed at their own pace. We try to understand what the teachers, the administrators and parents want to do, and then give them some tools – new software applications – to make that easier. Once you're using the Internet, then students can access their work anytime: they're not restricted to a 9am-3pm schedule.

'We provide equipment at community centres, libraries and museums, which can become access points, and we encourage them to keep schools open in the evenings. In Cincinnati we also outfitted a "parents room" at the school and a community centre in the public housing network.'

Parents – many unable to afford a PC – can use the IT centre to 'chat' on-line to teachers at any time. Each teacher maintains their own web pages, accessible by parents. The scheme has increased parental involvement by 80 per cent, according to project co-ordinator Anne Clarke. 'Teachers can't run and hide from parents now.'

Fair Share 2: Leeds United

Numeracy, literacy, ICT skills and football are brought together in a scheme to help underperforming pupils

Community United, run by Leeds United Football Club, was one of the first projects in the Government's Playing for Success initiative. It was opened in October by David Blunkett, and its premises are under the South Stand.

Emma Stanford, the club's community affairs manager, says: 'The directors of the club wanted to put something back into the community, and worked on the concept of Community United with the local education authority. It happens to be an area of Leeds that's earmarked for social regeneration funding, and levels of attainment in local schools are not as high as they'd like them to be.

'The Playing For Success scheme is funded by the club, the city council, and the DfEE. It's basically a study support project linking education and football, and it covers literacy, numeracy and ICT skills. We have an ex-headteacher and tutor-mentors from the University of Leeds. Our shirt sponsor, Packard-Bell, donated 20 PCs, and Planet On-line supplied Internet connectivity; other sponsors are Ikea, Kenco and McDonald's. We're open from 3.30 to 7.30 Monday to Friday, and on Saturday mornings, and work with kids aged 9-13 from 16 local schools.

'We have a cybercafe with Internet access, an IT suite and an integrated learning classroom, where we use Success-Maker. The Ikea look is more exciting than school, and the kids love to be involved with footballers: they run to get here. The centre is used by other young people and adults: we have half-term projects for families. It's the whole picture that's important.'

Fair Share 3: Laptop Scheme

A Cambridgeshire school is using a subsidised portables scheme to encourage families to embrace ICT at home

Sawtry Community College aims to create 'a connected learning community' that involves local children and their parents, the library, local businesses and everyone else.

It has a registered IT For All Centre, a Business Innovation Centre (rented to local companies as part of the DfEE's Technologies for Training service) and runs a training company called Multitask.

It is also one of the 28 British schools taking part in Microsoft's Anytime, Anywhere Learning (AAL) pilot using portable computers (500 more schools are joining this month).

Alan Stevens, Sawtry's vice-principal and the head of Multitask, says: 'We started experimenting with portable computers because we were conscious that we couldn't keep building more and more computer suites – classrooms with 15 computers installed. That's a very expensive model when the computes get limited use.

'With portables, we can use any classroom as a computer room, particularly now we've got a wireless network, which is attached via an ISDN line to the Internet. With the wireless network, we can also create a networked community. If we decide to take it off site, it has a range of about 17km, so families will be able to use the network at home without running up a phone bill.'

The AAL scheme involved 24 Year 8 students using Fujitsu note-book computers. About half the families have bought computers for home use, and the school has also

piloted leasing and renting out portables at a heavily subsidised £29 a month. Those unable to afford it received financial help.

Steven adds: 'It's no use saying the school can afford it, or local businesses, or parents can afford it. In a connected learning community, every partner has a budget, but no one partner can afford to run the scheme on its own. We all have to put something into the pot'.

Fair Share 4: After School

Futurekids offers host schools free use of its computers by day – and runs catch-up IT coaching classes by night

Futurekids supplies tuition in ICT to a wide age range from tiny tots to adults, for a fee: typically £150 for 12 one-hour lessons. The franchise operation started in the US about 15 years ago and now operates in more than 75 countries. It has 15 learning centres in the UK from Southampton to Edinburgh.

Richard Woolf, education director of Futurekids and a former teacher, says: 'A lot is being made of ICT in schools but often it's been badly planned. About half our pupils have computers at home, but often they're not used other than as games machines. At our after-school class they are taught to use them properly.

'We're setting up centres with one or two schools where we supply computers that are free for the schools to use during the day. Not only do children from that school come to classes but their brothers and sisters and friends from other schools. Our programmes start from the age of three and we do a lot of work with key stage 4 courses.

'We also run courses, two hours a day, in the summer. We license our curriculum to schools, and we'll give them some initial training: it's a complete package for ICT. Parents are using our facilities because they feel their children are not getting the skills they require in school. Some of them take second jobs to pay for it. We don't have assisted places: Futurekids is an "enrichment activity", like extra gym or swimming classes.'

Internet safety quiz for kids

Information from the National Center for Missing & Exploited Children (NCMEC)

Questions

1. *As I travel through 'Cyberspace', information I should never give out to someone I meet on-line is:*

a. the names of my favourite books and movies.

b. my real name, address, telephone number, the school I attend, or my photograph.

c. the name of my pet.

2. *If someone sends me an inappropriate message/material, I should:*

a. never reply to these messages and tell my parents, so that they can notify our on-line service provider.

b. keep it a secret.

c. reply to the message and ask the sender to stop sending me messages.

3. *If someone I meet on-line asks me to keep a secret from my parents I should:*

a. keep the secret because they are my 'cyber friend'.

b. tell all of my friends, because it's hard for me to keep a secret.

c. tell my parents, because no one should ever ask me to keep secrets from my parents.

4. *If someone is on my e-mail 'buddy list', 'friend list', or 'contact list' and I only know that person on-line, he or she is:*

a. my friend and someone I can trust.

b. the person he or she claims to be.

c. someone I should be cautious about, because I don't know him or her well.

5. *As I travel through 'Cyberspace', I should never:*

a. take a break and have a snack.

b. use the Internet to help me with my homework.

c. agree to meet someone in person who I have met on-line.

6. *The 'CyberTipline' is:*

a. a cool, new video game.

b. my on-line source to report child-sexual exploitation.

c. a web site where I can find information about UFOs.

Answers

1. *Answer: B*
I should always remember never to give out personal information in e-mails or to web sites, even if they're offering free merchandise, without checking with my parents first. I should also let my parents know about anything unusual or inappropriate that I discover while I'm on-line.

2. *Answer: A*
I need to let my parents know right away if I get messages that make me feel frightened or confused, so that they can let our on-line service provider know. I will not respond to these messages, and it isn't my fault if I get a message like that.

3. *Answer: C*
No one I meet on-line should ask me to keep secrets or do things that I wouldn't ordinarily do. It's easy to be anonymous on-line, and that's why I need to let my parents know who my 'cyber friends' are.

4. *Answer: C*
Just because people say they're my buddy, doesn't mean that they are. I should also be careful not to use screen names that give out personal information about me, because that may make it easier for someone to pretend to be my friend.

5. *Answer: C*
I should always tell my parents if anything bothers me about someone I meet on-line or if someone is asking for information about me.

I should let my parents know if I am confused about how the information is going to be used, so that they can contact our on-line service provider.

I should always tell my parents if someone I meet on-line wants to meet me in person, and I should <u>never</u> agree to meet someone in person who I have met on-line.

6. *Answer: B*
I can report anything that is threatening or involves child pornography to the CyberTipline by visiting their web site at www.cybertipline.com They will ask questions about what happened and give my parents and me information about people who can help me.

Safety on the internet

Information from The Children's Partnership

Web safety

Positive benefits for your child
- Access rich educational and cultural resources (text, sounds, pictures, and video) otherwise unavailable to most people.
- Obtain up-to-the-minute information.
- Improve ability to understand and evaluate information.
- Stay informed by accessing your community and school Web sites.
- Play fun and educational games.
- Learn educational skills useful in future jobs.

Danger/risks
- Easy-to-find sites with sexually explicit images and text.
- Easy-to-find sites promoting hatred, bigotry, violence, drugs, cults, and other things not appropriate for children.
- Inaccurate, misleading and untrue information.
- No restrictions on marketing products such as alcohol and tobacco to children.
- Marketing that deceptively collects personal information from kids in order to sell products to them or their parents.
- Requests for personal information for contests, surveys, etc., that are used in unauthorised ways.
- Easy access to games with excessive violence and gender stereotypes.

Parenting tips
- Keep computer in family area to better monitor your child's activity.
- Regularly spend time on-line with your child to learn about his or her interests and activities.
- Teach your child to end any experience on-line when he or she feels uncomfortable or scared by pressing the back key, logging off, and telling a trusted adult as soon as possible.
- Establish an atmosphere of trust and understanding with your child by not blaming him or her for uncomfortable on-line experiences.
- Discuss the difference between advertising and educational or entertaining content and show your child examples of each.
- Show your child the difference between sources of information that are credible and those that are not.
- Teach your child to never give out personal information unless he or she has your permission and you know how and by whom the information will be used.
- Establish strict rules for ordering products (and then monitor credit card bills).
- 'Talk back' to Internet Service Providers and content creators to let them know what you want and expect from them in keeping kids safe on-line.

What parental control tools can do
- Block access to materials (text and pictures) identified as inappropriate for kids.*
- Permit access only to materials specifically approved as safe for kids.*
- Allow you to specify what types of materials are appropriate for your child.
- Help you monitor your child's activity on the Internet by storing names of sites and/or snapshots of material seen by your child on the computer for you to view later.
- Allow you to set different restrictions for each family member.
- Limit results of an Internet search to content appropriate for kids.
- Block advertising that appears at the top of a Web page.
- Enforce time limits set by parents.
  * Each control tool determines whether materials are 'inappropriate' or 'safe for kids' differently. Make sure you ask what criteria the tool uses and how the evaluation process works; then check out the tool yourself.

Chat safety

Positive benefits for your child
- Develop relationships with children and adults around the world.
- Talk to kids and teens with similar interests and concerns, in rooms specifically for kids that are monitored closely by adults.
- Communicate instantaneously with family, friends, teachers, community leaders, etc.

Danger/risks
- Offensive language and adult conversation.
- Because of its interactive nature, the most likely activity on-line through which children will encounter people who want to harm them.
- Too much time on-line, which limits a child's well-rounded development by taking the place of friends, schoolwork, sports and other activities.

Parenting tips
- Accompany your child in chat rooms until he or she learns your safety rules.
- Teach your child to never give out personal information such as his or her name or address, school name or address, or anything else that is personally identifying.
- Explain that people are not always who they say they are.
- Set a rule that your child never arranges an in-person meeting without you present.
- Limit your child to specific chat rooms or consider blocking out chat entirely.

What parental control tools can do
- Allow access only to monitored chat rooms or block access to all chat rooms.
- Block private messages between a child and another user.
- Limit your child's ability to give out personal information.
- The above is an extract from The Children's Partnership (TCP) web site http://www.childrenspartnership.org
© 1998 The Children's Partnership

Don't jump too soon

Giving toddlers a computer may do more harm than good, reports Jim McClellan

If you have not yet bought your child a multi-media PC, are you stunting his or her education? After all, even the Prime Minister regularly suggests that computers will save our schools and boost our children's brains. And the computer business bolsters these arguments with programs promising kids a 'head start'.

But will educational software really help your child succeed at school? Some critics suggest not. In fact, some say that used in the wrong way, computers can actually hinder educational development. That's the thesis advanced by the American educational psychologist Jane Healy. Her new book, *Failure to Connect*, argues we need to look more closely at the claims made for computers and educational software.

Healy is no kneejerk luddite. Indeed, she admits to having been a 'techno-pusher'. But three years' research in schools has changed her mind. Her basic argument, very simplified, is that children under seven don't really need to be exposed to computers at all.

Many parents believe that if toddlers are sat in front of a PC, they will get used to computers and this will inevitably pay off later. Healy suggests all these parents will get is a lot of dribble on their keyboard.

She shows that children who played with computers only after the age of seven had no problem picking up the basics quickly and, all other things being equal, did not lag behind children who had been clicking away since they were in nappies. Beyond that, Healy says, too much mouse and screen time can harm young children, especially if it takes the place of more traditional forms of play – playing with blocks, singing and dancing. 'There is some evidence here that the creativity scores of pre-schoolers using this kind of "accelerative software" dropped by 50 per cent in a short time.'

Healy blames the marketing for parents' belief in the power of the PC. 'In America we seem to see machines as the solution to everything. Is the purpose of raising a child to produce a product that can compute faster than anybody else or is it to raise a thinking, caring, reflective human being?

'They're not going to become the latter from working with today's software, I promise you. Parents should be aware that the people who design the software by and large are not the people who know anything about child development.'

Healy says she has been offered consultancy work by computer companies but always refuses. After *Failure to Connect*, it seems unlikely she'll get too many more calls.

The under-fives market is seen as a significant growth area by educational software firms. Many are targeting ever younger customers. Last year saw the appearance of 'lapware' (renamed 'droolware' by critics), software aimed at children sometimes as young as nine months. The best-known title, Knowledge Adventure's *Jump Start Baby*, was published in the US in July and in six months sold 50,000 copies.

Renamed *Jump Ahead Baby* for the UK market, it is expected to do just as well here. Verna Harvey, its producer, says the program – which offers a point and click (or bash and crash) version of the things offered by books and puzzles (naming of body parts and clothes, simple peek-a-boo games) – isn't meant to replace books and is meant to be used by parent and child together, But do babies really need programs like this?

'I don't think they need it but I don't think it hurts,' she says. 'We actually took the cue from the parents. They wanted a product like this.'

Is she backing away from the implication in the Jump Ahead name for this software? 'As a producer of children's educational software, I'm very keen that we don't have pretentions or make claims that are unreasonable. We don't want to suggest that if you don't buy this, your children are not going to do well in school, not going to get into college and not going to lead productive lives. That would be inappropriate.'

The Jump Ahead title has been criticised by the independent Parents Information Network. Though PIN wrote the Parent's Guide included with the program, it told Knowledge Adventure the Jump Ahead tag carried a misleading message and suggested dropping it. That it remains is 'regrettable', says PIN's director Jacquie Disney. She is sceptical about any educational benefit from such programs. 'Say you have a toddler in a computer-literate family – it's worth having a piece of software for them so that there's something there that they can have a go with. But on any other level it's a complete nonsense.'

Healy particularly dislikes the American 'Jump Start' tag and argues its mechanistic overtones imply children are machines that needs to be started up. 'It's hard to keep a child from learning what it needs to learn at a certain age. Not only does the child's brain not need to be jump-started, it can be really seriously damaged by adult efforts to interfere mechanistically with this process.'

She seems most worried about children using computers for long periods on their own. It's better if they use them with a responsive adult. Much the same goes for TV, she suggests, where even a bad programme can be a good learning experience if an adult adds some critical context. Healy dismisses the idea computers are inherently better than TV. Both can be equally mind-numbing if used in the wrong way.

Response to her book has been good, Healy says. 'Saying children under seven don't even need to be on computers is really heresy over here. It's very interesting that the most technologically savvy people are the ones who have supported the thesis most strongly.'

Healy does emphasise the benefits of computer use by older children. Though she is less con-vinced by edutainment games (they are too often badly designed), she is enthusiastic about the guided use of simulation programs like *SimCity*. She also stresses the value of computer use for children with physical handicaps.

Because many parents will still buy software for toddlers, Healy says: 'I do give guidelines. If you have to do this, at least make sure it's not going to be stifling their imagination or shortening their attention span. Make sure that serious limits are placed on the time and that the child gets outdoor play.' It sounds like common sense, though there is evidence that some parents are so intoxicated by PCs that they are forcing their children to use them.

For all her criticisms, Healy remains enthusiastic about the educational potential of computers. 'I still have great hope,' she con-cludes. 'I think we will use this stuff constructively. But this is a perfect time to stand back and say, what are we doing and why are we doing it? I

would advise the UK to do that and not to respond to the blandishments of your politicians and your pro-moters who have something to gain just by saying something trendy.'

PIN points

The Parents Information Network (PIN), set up in 1994 in response to growing media hype about compu-ters, offers advice on buying a computer and how best to use it at home to back up school work.

It reviews all educational software published in the UK, though PIN director Jacquie Disney points out that educational benefits can come from programs not specifically aimed at children. For example, a word processing package can help to develop writing skills. Call: 0891 633 644. E-mail: post@pin-parents.com. Visit: www.pin-parents.com

PIN recommends: for under-fives, Knowledge Adventure's *Adiboo*. The I Can Read and I Can Count features offer simple games for numeracy and literacy.

Broderbund's *Carmen Sandiego* games and *The Logical Journey Of The Zoombinis* (a charming maths adventure) do the best job of integrating learning with game and entertainment elements.

For children around 10: Dorling Kindersley's *Pinball Science*, the latest CD-Rom from David Macaulay, author of *The Way Things Work*; and Disney Interactive's *Maths Quest With Aladdin*.

Failure to Connect by Jane Healy is published in America by Simon and Schuster ($25) and is available from on-line bookshops.

• First published in *The Guardian*, January, 1999.   ©*Jim McClellan*

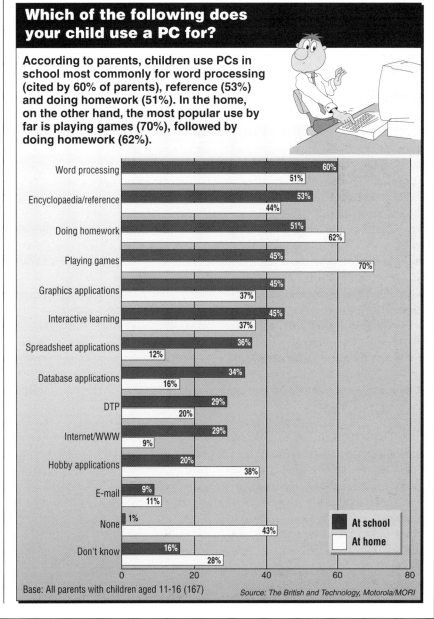

Which of the following does your child use a PC for?

According to parents, children use PCs in school most commonly for word processing (cited by 60% of parents), reference (53%) and doing homework (51%). In the home, on the other hand, the most popular use by far is playing games (70%), followed by doing homework (62%).

	At school	At home
Word processing	60%	51%
Encyclopaedia/reference	53%	44%
Doing homework	51%	62%
Playing games	45%	70%
Graphics applications	45%	37%
Interactive learning	45%	37%
Spreadsheet applications	36%	12%
Database applications	34%	16%
DTP	29%	20%
Internet/WWW	29%	9%
Hobby applications	20%	38%
E-mail	9%	11%
None	1%	43%
Don't know	16%	28%

Base: All parents with children aged 11-16 (167)   *Source: The British and Technology, Motorola/MORI*

Families switch off television to surf the Internet

By Robert Uhlig,
Technology Correspondent

Personal computers have changed the nature of British family life, dominating dinner-table conversation and challenging television as the favoured entertainment, says a report today.

The two-year study of 500 households reveals a snapshot of domestic life where family members vie to surf the Internet, and where computers have become a more popular topic of conversation than football, relationships, sex and hobbies. With one in four households owning a computer – more than those with satellite television or a mobile phone – the home computer is usurping the dog as man's best friend.

Although television just beats the computer for popularity at home, the average PC owner spends more than seven hours a week at the keyboard.

From 6pm to 8pm, families with computers are more likely to be in front of a monitor than watching soap operas such as *Coronation Street* and *EastEnders*.

Richard Taversham of Microsoft, which commissioned the study, said: 'The home PC is no longer the preserve of the well-off or the highly PC-literate. People spend more time with their computer than most other domestic activities, such as cooking, eating at home, reading, gardening, exercising or doing housework.'

The study is the most detailed examination yet of British attitudes to home computers. It contradicts previously held beliefs that computers have become the preserve of the young. Opinion Research International found that the over-60s spend more time on their home computers than any other age groups and talk more about computers than anyone else.

Twenty years ago, children were caught reading under the bedclothes or listening to the radio while their parents expected them to be sound asleep. Today, they sneak out of bed to play on the computer, according to the study which found that more than a third of under-10s were caught using the home computer after 10pm.

More than two-thirds of computer owners use their machine for word-processing, with over half admitting to playing computer games. One in three school-age children do their homework electronically, although girls are more likely to do so than boys.

The Nowaks, from Forest Hill, south London, are among the 20 per cent of families who have two or more home computers. Stefan Nowak, a computer consultant, said: 'They have enabled me to work from home and, in our family, the computer has become the primary source of entertainment instead of television. My eldest son, Aleks, is more likely to spend the evening playing games or on the Internet than watching television.'

© *Telegraph Group Limited, London 1998*

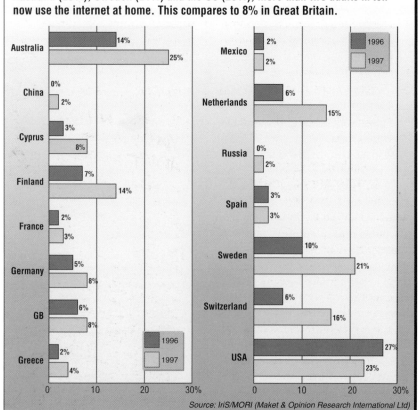

Access at home

While in most countries the workplace is still the preferred usage venue (for cost and speed reasons), home use has nearly doubled in several countries. In Australia (25%), Sweden (21%) and the US (23%), more than two adults in ten now use the internet at home. This compares to 8% in Great Britain.

Australia — 14% (1996), 25% (1997)
China — 0% (1996), 2% (1997)
Cyprus — 3% (1996), 8% (1997)
Finland — 7% (1996), 14% (1997)
France — 2% (1996), 3% (1997)
Germany — 5% (1996), 8% (1997)
GB — 6% (1996), 8% (1997)
Greece — 2% (1996), 4% (1997)
Mexico — 2% (1996), 2% (1997)
Netherlands — 6% (1996), 15% (1997)
Russia — 0% (1996), 2% (1997)
Spain — 3% (1996), 3% (1997)
Sweden — 10% (1996), 21% (1997)
Switzerland — 6% (1996), 16% (1997)
USA — 27% (1996), 23% (1997)

Source: IriS/MORI (Maket & Opinion Research International Ltd)

What is Internet addiction?

Information from the Illinois Institute for Addiction Recovery (IIAR)

What is Internet addiction?

Internet addiction is described as an impulse control disorder which does not involve use of an intoxicating drug and is very similar to pathological gambling.

Signs of Internet addiction include the following:

- Preoccupation with the Internet. (Thoughts about previous on-line activity or anticipation of the next on-line session.)
- Use of the Internet in increasing amounts of time in order to achieve satisfaction.
- Repeated, unsuccessful efforts to control, cut back, or stop Internet use.
- Feelings of restlessness, moodiness, depression or irritability when attempting to cut down use of the Internet.
- On-line longer than originally intended.
- Jeopardised or risked loss of significant relationships, job, educational or career opportunities because of Internet use.
- Lies to family members, therapist, or others to conceal the extent of involvement with the Internet.
- Use of the Internet as a way to escape from problems or to relieve a dysphoric mood (e.g., feelings of hopelessness, guilt, anxiety, depression).

Problems caused by Internet addiction

Internet addiction results in personal, family, academic, financial and occupational problems that are characteristic of other addictions.

Impairment of real-life relationships which are disrupted as a result of excessive use of the Internet. Internet addicts spend more time in solitary seclusion and spend less time with real people in their lives.

Arguments may result due to the volume of time spent on-line. Internet addicts may attempt to conceal the amount of time spent on-line, which results in distrust and the disturbance of quality in once stable relationships.

Financial problems may occur due to the significant amount of time spent on-line and the service provider charges. Common financial issues are large bills for use of some services, the telephone connection charges and telephone bills for calls made to 'friends' in chat rooms. Other financial charges may include a connection with compulsive spending/shopping. Internet addicts may choose to shop on-line and credit card charges for purchases may become high. Also, a connection with gambling exists with the availability of on-line casinos.

What makes the Internet addictive?

Some Internet users may develop an emotional attachment to on-line friends and activities they create on their computer screens. Internet users may enjoy aspects of the Internet that allow them to meet, socialise and exchange ideas through the use of chat rooms or 'virtual communities'. These communities allow

the person the means to escape from reality and seek out means to fulfil unmet emotional and psychological needs, which are more intimate and less threatening than real-life relationships.

Some Internet addicts may also create on-line personas where they are able to alter their identities and pretend to be someone other than themselves. The highest risk for creation of a secret life are those who suffer from low self-esteem, feelings of inadequacy, and fear of disapproval from others. Such negative self concepts lead to clinical problems of depression and anxiety.

There is help for Internet addiction. The Illinois Institute for Addiction Recovery at Proctor Hospital provides assessment and treatment services for the Internet addict. Counsellors trained in the identification and treatment of Internet addiction provide professional assessments to determine if addiction to the Internet exists and placement into a level of care for treatment.

A free, confidential assessment may be scheduled by calling the Illinois Institute for Addiction Recovery at Proctor Hospital at + 1 309 691 1055 or + 1 800 522 3784.

This information is provided as a community education service about professional issues and is not a substitute for individual consultation. Advice on individual problems should be obtained through a professional. All personal and medical information provided to IIAR and its staff is held in strict confidence. This information will not be disclosed to any person or organisation without the written consent of the patient or guardian.

• The above information is from the Addiction Recovery Centre web site which can be found at http://www.addictionrecov.org/
© *Illinois Institute for Addiction Recovery (IIAS)/Proctor Hospital, 1998*

The Internet addiction test

How do you know if you're already addicted or rapidly tumbling toward trouble? Everyone's situation is different, and it's not simply a matter of time spent on-line. Some people indicate they are addicted with only twenty hours of Internet use, while others who spent forty hours on-line insist it is not a problem to them. It's more important to measure the damage your Internet use causes in your life. What conflicts have emerged in family, relationships, work, or school? Let's find out. This is a simple exercise to help you in two ways: i) If you already know or strongly believe you are addicted to the Internet, this guide will assist you in identifying the areas in your life most impacted by your excessive Net use; and ii) if you're not sure whether you're addicted or not, this will help determine the answer and begin to assess the damage done. Remember when answering, only consider the time you spent on-line for non-academic or non-job related purposes.

To assess your level of addiction, answer the following questions using this scale:
1 = Not Applicable or Rarely. 2 = Occasionally. 3 = Frequently. 4 = Often. 5 = Always

1. How often do you find that you stay on-line longer than you intended?

2. How often do you neglect household chores to spend more time on-line?

3. How often do you prefer the excitement of the Internet to intimacy with your partner?

4. How often do you form new relationships with fellow on-line users?

5. How often do others in your life complain to you about the amount of time you spend on-line?

6. How often do your grades or school work suffer because of the amount of time you spend on-line?

7. How often do you check your e-mail before something else that you need to do?

8. How often does your job performance or productivity suffer because of the Internet?

9. How often do you become defensive or secretive when anyone asks you what you do on-line?

10. How often do you block out disturbing thoughts about your life with soothing thoughts of the Internet?

11. How often do you find yourself anticipating when you will go on-line again?

12. How often do you fear that life without the Internet would be boring, empty, and joyless?

13. How often do you snap, yell, or act annoyed if someone bothers you while you are on-line?

14. How often do you lose sleep due to late-night log-ins?

15. How often do you feel preoccupied with the Internet when off-line, or fantasise about being on-line?

16. How often do you find yourself saying 'just a few more minutes' when on-line?

17. How often do you try to cut down the amount of time you spend on-line and fail?

18. How often do you try to hide how long you've been on-line?

19. How often do you choose to spend more time on-line over going out with others?

20. How often do you feel depressed, moody, or nervous when you are off-line, which goes away once you are back on-line?

Your Score:

Results:
After you've answered all the questions, add the numbers you selected for each response to obtain a final score. The higher your score, the greater your level of addiction and the problems your Internet usage causes. Here's a general scale to help measure your score:

20 – 49 points: You are an average on-line user. You may surf the Web a bit too much at times, but you have control over your usage.

50 - 79 points: You are experiencing occasional or frequent problems because of the Internet. You should consider their full impact on your life.

80 – 100 points: Your Internet usage is causing significant problems in your life. You should evaluate the impact of the Internet on your life and address the problems directly caused by your Internet usage.

After you have identified the category that fits your total score, look back at those questions for which you scored a 4 or 5. Did you realise this was a significant problem for you? For example, if you answered 4 (often) to Question #2 regarding your neglect of household chores, were you aware of just how often your dirty laundry piles up or how empty the refrigerator gets?

Say you answered 5 (always) to Question #14 about lost sleep due to late-night log-ins. Have you ever stopped to think about how hard it has become to drag yourself out of bed every morning? Do you feel exhausted at work? Has this pattern begun to take its toll on your body and your overall health? Has your relationship been hurt because of Internet addiction or a cyberaffair? Then read our exclusive new booklet, *Infidelity Online: An Effective Guide to Rebuild your Relationship after a Cyberaffair*.

If your marriage or relationship has been damaged by a cyberaffair then read *Caught in the Net* to find the help you need. This book outlines the trauma of being a cyberwidow and shows you proven strategies on how to communicate with your partner to save your relationship.

• The above is an extract from the web site of The Center For On-Line Addiction, which can be found at http://www.netaddiction.com/

© The Center For On-Line Addiction

The Which? Online Annual Internet Survey

Foreword

Fact: the Internet is the fastest growing communications medium ever. Of course, that statement won't come as any surprise to most industry pundits today. But for British consumers, many of whom had never heard of the Internet as recently as two years ago, it can be jarring.

The Internet is a revolution of sorts, and revolutions, no matter how beneficial in the long run, scare people. Should consumers be scared of this one?

Initially, we at Which? Online were surprised at the level of fear and concern expressed by respondents in this survey. They are worried about credit card fraud, on-line addiction, computer viruses and apparently freely available pornography. In many cases, they feel that the very fabric of their lives is threatened by the Internet – their families, their high streets, even national security. Is this an overreaction? Most probably. Is it unfounded? Maybe not.

It is easy to see where consumers get these stories – they're covered nearly every day in the popular press. It is the responsibility of the Internet industry to educate consumers about the reality of the 'wired world' and to make it as easy and attractive as possible for them to sample it for themselves. Clearly, this is not happening.

So, let me make a start. First of all, the scares. Fraud, pornography, viruses, addiction. Yes, they are a part of the Internet but a very small part indeed. Often, as with pornography, you have to actively seek it out rather than it finding and entrapping you and your unsuspecting child, as goes the popular myth. Credit card fraud, during on-line transactions, is also much less common than one might imagine. In my years in the business, I have met very few who have suffered a loss on-line. There is no more risk with on-line purchases than there is with

By Alan Stevens, Editor, Which? Online

any other type of credit card transaction. And, if you are buying from a UK-based Web site, existing consumer law protects you.

The fact of the matter is that all these things – even at their most apocalyptic – are far outweighed by the benefits that the Internet offers consumers. Users know this; two out of three in this survey claimed that the Internet had improved the overall quality of their lives. Even the most hardened of sceptics is likely to become an enthusiast once on-line.

Although today's user profile is of a young, affluent male, the Internet can become, if not a life-saver, certainly a time-saver for many other niches of the population who currently view it as irrelevant to their needs. Such as the 'grey', over-55 market, the fastest growing sector of the Internet population in the United States. Here, only 2% of over-55s are connected. They think they're too old and that it will be too difficult to learn how to use the technology. In fact, it can be very easy and it will become easier still.

At Which? On-line, the average age of our subscribers is 46 and we have many in their 50s, 60s, 70s and older. These people want to keep in touch with family who do not live locally and make new friends, they have a reasonable income and plenty of time for such leisure pursuits.

In the Internet, they find not only a service, but a real community that meets their needs; one in which they can find and exchange information that helps solve everyday problems.

If the Internet market is to continue to grow, we in the industry need to attract more people like these subscribers. If we are to attract them, we must take our responsibility to educate very seriously indeed.

Consumers today harbour many fears and misconceptions about the Internet; this is only the start of the problem. This research demonstrates the incredible lack of understanding about the most basic workings of the Internet – what it's used for, how one gets on-line, and how much it costs. We need to make these things crystal clear if the bulk of British consumers – 30 million of whom currently brand themselves 'never-users' – are ever to welcome the revolution.

Executive summary

User profile:

- Approximately 14% of Britons – some eight million individuals – are using the Internet today.
- Users have a distinct profile. They tend to be male, under 35, living in the South, more affluent, employed, with no children living in the household.
- Age is one of the biggest determinants in Internet usage. Over half of users are under 35 whereas only one in twenty is over 55 years of age.

About the users

- Half of the current user population signed on within the past year. As dial-up Internet connections have been available since about 1993, this shows a dramatically increasing rate of adoption, with nearly as many users coming on-line in the past year as in the previous four years.
- Three out of four users are on-line for less than five hours a week, although five per cent admitted to spending 20 or more hours on-line weekly. One in ten agreed that they spent too much time on the Internet.
- Education and business purposes were the biggest draws initially bringing users on-line. Once on-line, social activities, such as emailing friends and family and accessing leisure information, proved to be popular regular uses of the Internet. Downloading software was also a regular activity for one in four respondents.
- Despite rosy predictions for the growth of e-commerce, on-line shopping is neither a draw for British consumers to get on-line nor an enticing activity once they are there. The vast majority (81%) have never bought anything over the Internet.
- If users could change one thing about the Internet, most of them would make it faster. Others would like to, amongst other things, reduce the cost, regulate it, improve the quality of the information and make it more user-friendly.
- Users do not see the Internet as a replacement for more traditional means of communication. Half still prefer face-to-face meetings as their choice of communication method, followed by 36% who prefer telephone conversations. E-mail has become much more popular than the postal service – nine per cent prefer it versus only one per cent who prefer the post.
- Two out of three users claimed that the Internet had improved their overall quality of life.
- The majority (87%) of users are happy with their Internet Service Providers (ISPs). Of the eight per cent who are unhappy, the main reasons given for their dissatisfaction were that the ISP's service was either too slow (49%) or too expensive (29%). They also complained about the poor quality of the Internet connection and insufficient or unhelpful customer support.

About the non-users

- Thirty per cent of non-users intend to become connected to the Internet at some stage, although 19% admitted that it would not be for at least another year.
- A worrying 61% of non-users, approximately 30 million individuals in the wider population, said that they never intend to go on-line. The number of never-users increases dramatically with age, with 85% of those over 55 saying they will never be connected to the Internet.
- Half of all non-users do not believe that the Internet is relevant to their needs, which is why they have not yet connected. A further 30% have resisted because of the cost and 16% because they are afraid of or do not understand the technology.
- A great deal of ignorance remains amongst non-users both about what is done on the Internet and

---

E-mail has become much more popular than the postal service – nine per cent prefer it versus only one per cent who prefer the post

---

about how it is used. One in four non-users did not even know that you need a computer to get on-line and the majority did not realise you need anything else. Only 37% knew that a telephone line was necessary. And only 27% and 9% respectively knew that either a modem or ISP was required.
- Nearly half of respondents had no idea how much Internet access costs. One in three non-users thought Internet service cost more than £15 per month, with one in ten believing that the cost exceeded £30 per month. In fact, most services cost far less than this, with many offering extended free trial periods or other discounts.

General attitudes

- Fears and misconceptions surrounding the Internet continue to abound, even amongst users. The biggest fear, held by 58% of all respondents, is that the Internet undermines the morality of the nation by making pornography and other illegal materials freely accessible.
- Nearly half of respondents believed that the Internet encourages fraudulent practices and one in three feared that it poses a threat to national security. Other institutions felt to be threatened are family life (feared by 22% of respondents), the high street (21%) and education. Only 16% thought that the Internet poses no threat at all.
- Only 13% of respondents said they would feel comfortable letting their children use the Internet unsupervised.
- Seventy-two per cent of respondents believed that the Internet should be regulated; just ten per cent said that it should not.
- Despite these concerns, the majority of respondents (75%) do believe that the Internet is here to stay and that it will become a vital part of the future of communications.

• The above information is from the Which? Online web site, which can be found at www.which.net

Spam

Information from the Police Notebook at the University of Oklahoma Department of Public Safety

Foreword

This article discusses unsolicited email, both commercial and non-commercial, and multi-level marketing schemes. While there are legitimate multi-level marketing programs in existence there are also so many illegal scams on the Internet, being sent out as unsolicited email, that it may be impossible for the average consumer to make any intelligent choice as to what 'offerings' are legitimate and what are not.

The old Latin phrase, *caveat emptor* (let the buyer beware), was never more true than today as applied to unsolicited commercial email offerings. Our only advice can be that if you would even consider reading or responding to email Spam that you read all you can about the illegal activities going on so you have a frame of reference when considering any offer which 'seems' to be legal. Remember, always: If it sounds too good to be true, it probably is.

Participation in many of the 'legitimate sounding' schemes currently being offered on the Internet will not only cost you money, but may subject you to serious civil and criminal liabilities.

Dealing with Spam

Your Internet Service Provider (ISP) usually can't take any action against Spam you receive, that you can't do more efficiently (and much more quickly) for yourself, unless the spammer is operating from one of your own ISP's accounts. Here are some advice and resources to help you deal with Spam, primarily related to how you can identify spammers and report them to someone who CAN take action.

What is Spam?

Spam is sending out many copies of the same unsolicited email (or Usenet) messages, usually for commercial advertising purposes, to persons who have had no prior dealings/relationship with the sender or the company he/she represents. It's also called UCE (Unsolicited Commercial E-Mail) and 'flooding'. The root of the term 'spam' comes from an old Monty Python song, Spam, where the word is repeated over and over again ('Spam, spam, spam, spam, spam . . . ') – which is what electronic Spam does: sends out the same message over and over again to many recipients, usually using one or more lists.

A spammer is someone who sends out Spam. If a spammer has your name on a list, you will often get many messages from him/her over a period of time, though none may show the same 'address' in the 'From:' field of the message since many spammers forge the FROM information to confuse the trail as to who actually sent out the information. Furthermore, if you're on a spammer's list, he/she may share that list with other spammers, which will add to your problems.

The term spamming is the act of sending Spam.

Classic commercial Spam may include come-ons such as 'Make Money Fast!' or 'Extra Holiday Cash!' or 'Mass Email Works!'

All you have to do is send them a few dollars and they'll share the secret of how to make easy money!

Often, that secret is how to sell the secret to other people. It's a variation of the classic pyramid scheme: a multi-level marketing 'program' built around people giving other people money in exchange for no real product other than the 'secret' of how to make money by getting other people to give you money for the secret of . . .

Why is Spam bad?

Other than that it's unsolicited, which you may not see as necessarily bad, the content of Spam mail is usually 'worthless, deceptive, and partly or entirely fraudulent'. Spammers are people (or people working for people) who want to separate you from your money, and make you pay them to do it.

How do I know who actually sent the Spam?

To know who is actually sending you Spam, you'll often have to view the 'full header' of the message. Many email clients don't show 'full header' information by default. However, it will usually have a option, which you can select, to allow you to view the full header information from the message. A full header shows the various hops the message took from its sender to you.

The sender's 'return address' shown in the normal 'FROM:' box on many readers may often be a forgery when dealing with Spam.

Many email clients have a method of storing 'stationary mail' or boilerplate text so it can be very easy to create and save a 'complaint template' for your future use.

Make your complaint letters polite, short, and to the point, and include the offending message (or at least part if it's long) and be sure it shows the full header information of the message.

© 1997, University of Oklahoma

Chain letters

Information from The Police Notebook at the University of Oklahoma Department of Public Safety

Just as we'd want to forward an urgent 'virus alert' we'd just received to all our friends, when someone receives an e-mail message telling of a brave little girl, dying of cancer, whose last wish is to receive the most e-mail messages in the world, they want to send it to their friends.

Resist the urge. Please.

At least, before you take any action regarding re-emailing a touching chain letter, check with someone you trust, or check it out yourself, to make sure it's just not one of many Internet hoaxes. And our best advice: Just say no to chain letters.

One of the most well-known e-mail chain letter hoaxes is the Jessica Mydek hoax. The first paragraphs of CIAC's 'Internet Chain Letters' page read:

- 'The Internet community is constantly being bombarded with chain letters in the form of e-mail messages. They claim all manner of warnings and dire notices of doom and gloom for your computer systems or for some poor soul somewhere, all of which will be saved if you just send this message on to all of your friends.
- 'Enter the world of the Internet chain letter. In the years before computers, chain letters were common and were sent by US mail and required a stamp. This limited the extent to which chain letters were passed on, because sending them involved a real, up-front cost in time to type the letters and money for stamps. The fact that most chain letters asked you to send a dollar to the top ten people in the chain caused most people to ignore them.
- 'Today, with the click of a button, a message can be forwarded to hundreds of people at no apparent cost to the sender. If each of the so-called good Samaritans sends the letter on to only ten other people (most send to huge mailing lists), the ninth resending results in a billion e-mail messages, thereby, clogging the network and interfering with the receiving of legitimate e-mail messages. Factor in the time lost reading and deleting all these messages and you see a real cost to organisations and individuals from these seemingly innocuous messages.
- 'Not only are these messages time consuming and costly, they may also be damaging to a person's or organisation's reputation as in the case of the Jessica Mydek and the American Cancer Society chain letters.'

Some chain letters are just a means to use the Internet to forward

---

'Today, with the click of a button, a message can be forwarded to hundreds of people at no apparent cost to the sender'

---

non-computer 'hoaxes'. By example, you can read about the great 'Kidney Harvest' hoax at several sites, including:

http://snopes.simplenet.com/horrors/robbery/kidney.htm

http://snopes.simplenet.com/horrors/robbery/kidney2.htm

Another problem with chain letters (however well meaning) particularly on the Internet via e-mail, is that they can develop 'a life of their own' completely separate from reality.

Take for example the case of Craig Shergold involving the Make-A-Wish foundation. This is a real boy who had a real brain tumour, but his tumour was successfully removed in 1991, and he's fully healed. And millions of e-mail letters still come in, six years later, despite pleas from the family and others to put a stop to the letters.

• The above is an extract from the Police Notebook web site at the Univeristy of Oklahoma Department of Public Safety, which can be found at http://www.ou.edu/oupd/

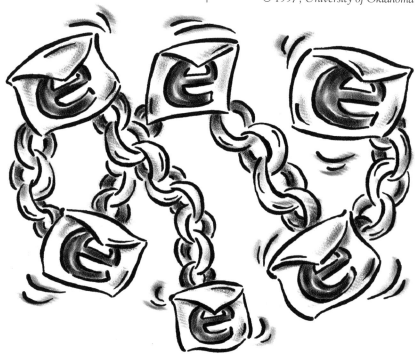

How to shake off that virus

Computer viruses used to affect mainly people who used pirated copies of computer games but the internet now allows viruses to spread across the world in a matter of minutes. According to internet services provider Star, whose system currently handles 10,000 e-mails per hour, 100 of them carry a virus.

A virus is a computer programme written to have a covert effect on computers. There are two types: the benign to frighten or amuse but not to do any real damage, and the malignant, which can cause all sorts of problems such as corrupting programs, deleting files or even stopping the computer from functioning.

Some viruses have the ability to self-replicate and propagate very quickly. The recent fright was at the outbreak of the new Melissa virus, which can infect Word 97 and Word 2000 documents and spread by sending itself to up to 50 users from the e-mail address book.

A more destructive virus called Chernobyl was created in 1998 to cause serious damage by modifying one of the main computer chips, thus preventing the computer from starting. In some cases the damage was so severe that the only way to start the computer again was to replace the machine's main circuit board.

So how can you protect your computer from becoming infected? One of the simplest methods is to stop downloading files from the Internet and loading computer programs when you are unsure about their origin.

Another method is to buy some anti-virus software. There are several manufacturers such as Network Associates, Quarterdeck, and Symantec, which produces the popular Norton AntiVirus.

Rob Murray

Virus checkers are good only if they are new. Five or six months old, and even the best is no longer primed to catch the latest round of mischief. Few of those on the market are likely to catch Melissa.

That is the one that produced such a scare recently though its main sin was to cause embarrassment.

It comes as attachments to e-mails most frequently headed 'Subject: Important Message From' and the name of the person whose computer relayed the virus.

Word documents created on an infected computer will contain the virus, too, and every time they are opened, the e-mail will be sent to 50 other people. But it is otherwise relatively benign since it causes no direct damage to a computer's memory or programs.

Several anti-virus software makers, including McAfee, Symantec, Trend Micro and Sophos, posted additions to their programs on their web sites to detect and reject the virus. People can also protect themselves by not opening e-mail attachments.

But even the latest protection program will lose its potency and need revision regularly.

One way to keep ahead of the vandals is to register after purchase

with the software company and subscribe to updates.

The latest version of Dr Solomon – now owned by Network Associates which also produces another of the leading brands, the McAfee virus checker – has © 1999 on the CD-Rom and the floppy disc.

When running, however, the dates of August and October 1998 are displayed. The company insists the versions available are nevertheless bang up to date, but the program warns users to renew it.

It does find and eliminate viruses and even rogue remnants of programming but it can slow down the computer. Updates are part of the package but there is little help in how to get them.

Michael Becket

The latest Norton anti-virus program can stay on the computer permanently, thus protecting the user from infection from e-mail attachments, downloaded files from the Internet, floppy discs, CDs, etc.

It also quarantines infected files until you decide what to do with them.

This stops the file infecting the computer, and ensures that the user does not accidentally pass infected files to other computers. Moreover, by using the Scan and Deliver facility you can send your quarantined files to Symantec AntiVirus research centre which will identify suspicious files.

Norton has launched the Live Update facility, which enables the user to download the latest virus definitions as often as once a week.

Norton AntiVirus 5.0 costs from £26 plus VAT, including 12 months' subscription to the live update service.

System requirements for Windows 95/98 are a 486 microprocessor or above, 8MB of memory, 24 MB of hard disc space and CD-ROM drive.

Rob Murray

Teen safety on the information highway

By Lawrence J. Magid

Whatever your age, the Internet is a great place to hang out. It's not only fun, but it lets you keep in touch with friends and family and provides an enormous amount of information. There are lots of great educational sites as well as places to keep up with your favourite sports, hobbies, music, and much more. If you're a teen, we probably don't need to sell you on the benefits of the Internet. Many of you know far more than your parents or even teachers about the wonders of cyberspace. If you're a parent, talk to your kids about 'the Net' and – if you need to learn more – see if they can help you. Either way, it's important for teens and parents to share knowledge. You have something to learn from each other – if not about the Internet, then about life in general, how to make good decisions, and how to look at information critically.

Cyberspace is like a big city. There are libraries, universities, museums, places to have fun, and plenty of opportunities to meet wonderful people from all walks of life. But, like any community, there are also some people and areas that you ought to avoid and others that you should approach only with caution.

By knowing the dangers and how to avoid them, you can take advantage of all the positive aspects of the Internet while avoiding most of its pitfalls.

If you're a teen or a parent of a teenager you might feel that you don't need the same restrictions and controls as younger kids. You may be right, but just because you're older doesn't mean that you're out of danger. Teenagers are actually more likely to get into trouble on-line than younger kids. Teens are more likely to explore out-of-the-way nooks and crannies of cyberspace, they're more

likely to reach out to people outside of their immediate peer groups and, sadly, they're more often preyed upon as victims by paedophiles and other exploiters.

How do I get into cyberspace?

There are lots of front doors to cyberspace, including Internet service providers and on-line services, that can provide you with an account that gives you access to everything on the public Internet. This includes web sites, e-mail, chat rooms, file libraries, discussion groups (called newsgroups), and lots of other services including the ability to listen to music and view videos.

An on-line service can, in some situations, exercise some control over the type of content and 'customer conduct' in its own areas, but the services have no control or jurisdiction over what takes place on the Internet as a whole. And even within their own areas, these services can't possibly police everything that happens. So, even if you're going on-line using one of these services, you're not completely protected from the larger dangers.

Before going into the dangers, let's put this into context. Millions

of teenagers go on-line every day, and most are safe. The way to stay safe is to understand the dangers and follow some simple rules to help you stay out of trouble. By following these rules you minimise the risks, but you can never completely eliminate all risks in life.

General risks

Situations and behaviour that make you feel uncomfortable

Not everything that can go wrong in cyberspace necessarily puts you in physical danger. There are web sites, newsgroups, chat rooms, and other places on-line that contain material that could make you feel uncomfortable. It could be material that's sexual and/or violent in nature. It could be material espousing hateful attitudes or discussing activities that you find repulsive or unpleasant. It really doesn't matter what it is. What does matter is that you have the right – and the tools – to instantly remove yourself from any area where you feel you shouldn't be.

Putting yourself in physical danger

The most serious risk you can face involves the possibility of someone hurting or exploiting you because of information that you post or someone else posts about you on-line or because of something you do or somewhere you go as a result of what you encounter on-line. The number of teens who are molested, abducted, or leave home as a result of contacts made on the Internet are relatively low, but when it happens the results can be tragic.

Giving up privacy or putting yourself or your family in financial risk

The Internet, like so many other places in this world, is home to people who would try to take money from you or your family or just pester you with unwelcome advertising and marketing material. Be especially wary of any 'get rich quick' schemes that promise to help earn you lots of money in your spare time. If something sounds 'too good to be true', it probably is.

Harassment

Not everyone in cyberspace minds their manners. When you're on-line, especially in chat rooms or bulletin boards, there is a chance that you'll get messages that are harassing, demeaning, or just plain mean. Don't take it personally. A message that is demeaning says a lot more about the sender than it does about the person who gets it. Ironically, even people who are nice in the 'real' world can forget their manners when they go on-line. The best thing to do if you encounter messages or people in chat rooms who are acting that way is to ignore them. Some messages, however, may constitute harassment, which is a crime under federal law. If someone sends you messages or images that are obscene, lewd, filthy, or indecent with the intent to harass, abuse, annoy, or threaten you, report it to your Internet service provider and the National Center for Missing and Exploited Children's Cyber-Tipline at www.missingkids.com/cybertip

Hurting others and getting into trouble

Avoid anything that might hurt people and risk getting yourself into trouble. You need to respect other people's privacy and avoid taking any actions that annoy, harass, or hurt other people. You are responsible for your behaviour on-line.

Risks by area

The web

Web sites give you the opportunity to read newspapers, tour museums, check out libraries, visit distant lands, play games, look at pictures, shop, or do research to help you with your homework. You can pursue your hobbies, plan vacations, and much more. There are millions of web sites on just about every topic imaginable.

Did you know?

Some web sites are wonderful, others are kind of dumb, and some contain so-called 'adult' images and other material that teens should avoid. Still others are violent, racist, sexist, and demeaning. Some of these sites contain material that can be disturbing, even for adults. If you wander into any of these areas, it's best to leave immediately by clicking on the Home icon, going to another site, or shutting down your browser.

Caution

In addition to displaying information, web sites sometimes ask you for information about yourself. The site may ask for your name, mailing address, e-mail address, and other information before it will let you in. It may entice you to provide information in exchange for sending you a promotional item or entering you in a contest. Never enter any information about yourself without first checking with your parents.

When you enter information on a web site or anyplace on the Internet, you're giving up a bit of your privacy. At best, your name will wind up in some database, probably to be used to sell you something now or later. At worst, it could be used to harm or exploit you. Just because a web site seems to be operated by a reputable organisation or individual doesn't mean that it necessarily is what it seems to be. Anyone – including creeps and criminals – can set up their own web site. So be extremely cautious before telling the 'web master' anything about yourself. This is especially true with sites that contain adult material.

Some teenagers have their own web sites or post material to web sites maintained by their school or an organisation. That's terrific, but if you do post something on the web, be sure never to include your home address, telephone number, or a photograph of yourself. If you do want people to be able to contact you through the web, just give an E-mail address.

Chat rooms

Chat rooms let you engage in a live conversation with people around the block or around the world. It's like being on a party line, only you type instead of talk. Everyone in the 'chat room' can see everything you type. The types of chat rooms vary depending on the service you're using. Some chat rooms are just open conversations. Everyone has a pretty much equal role. Some rooms are moderated where there is a 'speaker' who is leading the discussion and participants. Some rooms have chaperons or monitors who are responsible for maintaining order, but even in some of these rooms what you type is displayed immediately. The monitor can kick someone out of the room who is acting in an inappropriate manner, but he or she may be able to act only after the fact. The monitor can't, however, prevent you from going off to a private chat area with a person who might do you harm or typing information that could put you in danger.

Did you know?

Chat is probably the most dangerous area on the Internet for a couple of reasons. As with other areas of the Internet, you don't know who is there, so never say anything in a chat room that you wouldn't say in public.

It's not uncommon for people to make 'friends' in chat rooms. You enter a room; start a conversation with someone; and, before you know it you've established a relationship of sorts. That relationship could turn out OK, but there are some not-so-happy stories. Chat rooms are sometimes used by people to exploit others. To put it bluntly, chat rooms – especially those used by teenagers – are sometimes also used by paedophiles to find victims. Adults or even older teens seeking to exploit younger people don't necessarily tell the truth about who they are.

You might meet someone in a room who appears to be sympathetic and understanding and offers you wonderful advice and counsel. If the relationship remains strictly on-line, that could be OK as long as you're careful not to give out any personal information and you let your parents know.

Caution

It can be tempting to get together with someone you meet in a chat room, but remember – people are not always who they seem to be. The basic rules for on-line safety apply to all areas of the Internet, but they are especially important in chat areas. Never give out personal information, and never arrange a face-to-face meeting with someone you meet in a chat room without first checking with your parents.

Chat rooms are sometimes organised around topics, so avoid any topic area that makes you feel uncomfortable. But just because a chat room is designed around a particular topic doesn't mean that other topics aren't discussed. Even if the room is 'teens only', you have no way of knowing if everyone really is a teenager, so you still have to be on guard.

Be especially careful of chat rooms that get into subjects that might be associated with sex or cults or groups that practise potentially dangerous rituals. It might seem interesting or even fun to discuss actions that you might never consider engaging in, but some people who fantasise about things also like to carry them out.

Be suspicious of anyone who tries to turn you against your parents, teachers, or friends. They may have a hidden agenda.

On some services and web sites you can enter into a private chat area where you can arrange to meet friends. In some cases, those rooms are truly private. But in other cases they may be listed in a directory of rooms. If so, there is nothing to stop others from entering those rooms.

One trick to avoid harassment, especially for women and girls, is to choose a gender-neutral name – like

your initials or a word – to use in a chat room. It's fine to be cute or funny with the name you choose, but be sure it doesn't identify you and doesn't have any meaning or implication that might encourage others to bother you.

E-mail

E-mail is typically a one-to-one communications system. Just like regular mail, you write to someone and they can write back.

Did you know?

Increasingly, people and companies are using e-mail to send out messages to thousands of people at a time, encouraging them to buy something, do something, or visit a web site. The process, known as 'spamming', can be intrusive and annoying. Because e-mail is essentially free, 'spammers' can send out thousands or even millions of messages at little or no cost. Some use spamming to try to entice people to visit sexually explicit web sites.

Each e-mail message that you send and receive contains a return address. What many people don't realise is that the return address can be fake. So, just because you get a message from 'grandma @cottage.com' doesn't mean it's really from grandma. It could really be from 'wolf@bigfangs.com'. E-mail also contains other information called a 'header' that provides more information about who sent the message and where it came from. Understanding the header information can be difficult, but if you ever receive an e-mail message that is belligerent, threatening, or contains material that makes you feel un-

comfortable, you should report it to your Internet service provider and ask them to investigate where it came from. If the material appears to be illegal in nature, you should report it to the CyberTipline at www.missingkids.com/cybertip. Illegal material includes threats to your life or safety, threats to others, child pornography, and evidence of other crimes. NCMEC will refer this report to the appropriate federal law enforcement agencies.

Caution

Be careful how you respond to e-mail from people you don't know. Remember, the sender might not be who he or she seems to be. Never send a photograph of yourself or any personal information to someone you don't know. Also, e-mail can easily be copied and forwarded to others. So if you do send personal information to friends, be sure that they are willing to respect your privacy.

In general, it's best not to respond to spam mail or mail from someone you don't know. By responding, you are verifying to the sender that you have a valid e-mail address, and that information can be used to encourage a person who may send inappropriate e-mails or get you on even more lists. If you receive a message that contains material that is sexually explicit, violent, or advocates something that is illegal or simply makes you feel uncomfortable, show it to your parents and report that message to your Internet service provider. You can usually find that address on the service's main web page (www.servicename.com). When in doubt, report the message to postmaster@servicename.com (substitute the name of your service for 'servicename').

• This information is from *Teen Safety on the Information Highway* by Lawrence J. Magid. It is reprinted with permission of the National Center for Missing & Exploited Children (NCMEC).

Notes, advice and warnings

For kids on the Web

Sometimes somebody on the Net may ask you for information your parents may not want you to give out. Always remember, if thinking about doing something makes you feel uncomfortable, it's probably wrong. When in doubt, ask.

Along the same lines, if reading or looking at something on the Net makes you uncomfortable, don't look at it! The back button is your friend.

What if they want a password?

Before you can play some games on the Web, you may have to fill out a form that asks for your name or a nickname, and asks you to pick a password. This is a very good idea – you wouldn't want somebody else to go claiming your game scores, or making you look stupid by sending dumb messages that appear to come from you.

But:

If you already have a password at home or at school, pick a different one! Remember, your password is a secret, and any time you tell something to more than one other person (or computer), it's not a secret any more.

For some things, like a game on the World Wide Web, it's OK to use something easy to remember like a parent's first name. But if your reputation, your money, or your homework is at stake, play it safe and use something really weird that mixes numbers, upper- and lower-case letters, and maybe a bit of punctuation. Some people develop a system for coming up with passwords that are hard to guess but easy to remember. Just don't tell anyone else your system.

Keeping secrets

If you go around giving out different passwords to lots of places on the Web, you'll probably have to write them down somewhere. Do you have a box with a lock on it in your room? A diary? If you're on a Unix machine, you can make a file called my-secrets

that only you (or your system administrator) can read, by typing:

    touch my-secrets
    chmod og-rw my-secrets

You can make a whole private directory with the commands:

    mkdir Private
    chmod og-rwx Private

If you're not on a Unix machine, keep your secrets on a floppy disk and keep it with you.

If you *really* need to keep something secret, find out about encryption.

Warning!

Encryption is illegal in some parts of the world, and in any case may give your parents or system administrator the impression that you don't trust them.

Warning!

If you *do* decide to encrypt something, *don't forget your password!* If you forget your Unix password, your system administrator can give you another one. If you forget an encryption password, your data is gone for good.

What if they want my real name?

In some traditions (for example, some African and American Indian cultures, not to mention comic-book superheroes) people have a name

they use in public and another, secret name they tell to no one. The secret name has magical powers, and if anybody learns your secret name, you're in big trouble.

Some people think that the Net is that way. They use nicknames or handles, and don't tell anyone who they really are. As for me, I'm Steve Savitzky and my daughter is Katy, and I don't care who knows it, because anyone who wants to find out, can do it. But ask your parents what they think. And by all means, if you don't feel comfortable giving out your real name, don't.

In any case, treat your password as a secret name, and don't tell it to anybody!

What if they want my address?

This section applies to forms on the Web; e-mail is different.

Ask an adult to advise you on this one. They may be planning to send you e-mail or snail-mail trying to sell you something you don't need; your parents may object to this. You may have to look in a section labelled 'for parents' or 'for adults' to find out why they want your address; you may want a grown-up around when you do this.

If they don't ask for your street address it's almost certainly safe to tell them the rest – they may be

collecting information about where you're from, but at least they won't be sending you junk mail.

Also, if the people who want your address say they'll keep it a secret and won't sell their mailing list, you can probably trust them. But they can still send you junk mail, unless they say they won't. And many places will come right out and tell you that they'll send you a catalogue or a flier. (They'll probably send one every month, but that may be just what you want.) But if they don't tell you what they're going to do with the information they're asking for, ask them or assume the worst.

What if they want my phone number?

This section applies to forms on the Web; e-mail is different.

Asking for your phone number can be a sneaky way of finding out where you live, and they may call your parents trying to sell them stuff.

People who call other people on the phone and try to sell them stuff are called telemarketers (some people call them things I shouldn't write down where kids can read them); they usually call around dinnertime, which isn't very nice. If this happens, get the parent who's best at telling people off to write them a nasty letter.

What if it's too grown-up for me?

Just skip it and find something else to look at. What people find interesting changes as they grow up. Also, remember that there are millions of people on the Net, from almost every country and culture in the world. You're bound to be interested in different things, and offended by different things. Try to be tolerant.

Many adults have different opinions about what children, and even other adults, should be allowed to read, listen to, and look at. These opinions change with time, and vary from place to place. In Japan, people take baths together and don't worry about seeing each other naked. In some Muslim countries it's illegal for a woman to show her face in public. Some people think that certain kinds of books should be

burned, or at least banned. There is no agreement over which kinds of books. Others (like me) think that burning books is worse than burning people. Enough said?

What if they say things I disagree with?

Once again, there are lots of people and cultures on the Net. Many of the most vocal people have strongly-held opinions about controversial subjects, and try to bring other people to their way of thinking. This is sometimes a good thing – it can make you think about your own beliefs and opinions. It's a problem if someone gets obnoxious, insulting, or overly insistent.

By the way, an argument over beliefs, opinions, or preferences on the Net is called a 'religious argument' even when the subject isn't religion, which most people have enough sense not to argue about. Two of the most frequent arguments on the Net are over which of the PC or Macintosh is the better personal computer, and which of vi and emacs is the better text editor.

As my own mother used to tell me, 'it takes all kinds to make a world'. Sometimes I wish more people had mothers who told them that.

Also by the way, a rude or insulting message in e-mail or a newsgroup posting is called a 'flame'. Flaming is considered impolite. My mother also used to tell me, 'if you don't have anything nice to say, don't say anything at all'.

£££ What are they selling?

Many sites are trying to sell something. This is just like advertising on TV that's aimed at kids. What they really want you to do is pester your parents until they buy something for you.

There may also be an order form on the Web page. Don't use it!!! Usually the form asks for a credit-card number, so you'll have to ask your parents to place the order for you anyway. Chances are, they won't. The best thing to do is put the URL that describes the thing being sold onto your bookmark list, and e-mail the links to your parents about a month before Christmas or your birthday.

What if they send me e-mail?

Keypals and net friends are great! You can have friends all over the world, swap pictures and your favourite dessert recipes, and maybe even meet face to face some day. A couple of warnings are in order:

- Ask a parent to advise you about giving somebody you've just met in e-mail your real name (if it's not normally in your header), your phone number, or your address. If you're away at college be especially careful about this.
- Be prepared for a few surprises; not everyone you meet on the Net is exactly who they say they are. That 18-year-old girl who's been reading your poetry and advising you about how to get a boyfriend might be a 13-year-old boy who's hacked into his big sister's account, a 15-year-old girl trying to act grown-up, a lonely 50-year-old woman with kids your age, or (less likely, but not totally impossible) a criminal looking for potential victims. She may even be a politician or a journalist trying to find out how easy it is for criminals to meet kids on the Net.
- Be prepared for a certain amount of mistrust and suspicion, too. If somebody is mailing from a student account on a machine in a high school, you can be pretty sure about *them*, but they may not be so sure about *you*.

On the other hand, if you're introduced through somebody you both trust, you're probably safe, and less likely to be surprised. If two 6th grade classes in different parts of the world get together to exchange e-mail, for example, there are unlikely to be any impostors in the group.

The Web is also a good way to check up on people. If the person you're corresponding with has a Web page, take a look. If not, ask whether their school is on the Web, or any of their friends. If you know someone's last name and the city they live in (in the US), you can often find them in Switchboard, which gets its information from phone books.

What should I look out for?

If someone sends you e-mail and you haven't been introduced through your school, a parent, or a friend that you know personally (not just on-line), there are a few warning signs to watch out for.

- If they ask you not to tell your parents about them. Tell your parents right away!
- If they send you a gift. Ask yourself if you would take a gift like that from a stranger in a car.
- If they won't tell you much about themselves. Maybe they're not who they say they are.
- If they do tell you about themselves and it doesn't check out. Make sure you do check it out. If they tell you the name of the town they live in, look it up on a map. Ask them questions. Does their school have a Web page? If it doesn't all check out, that means they've been lying to you and will probably lie to you about other things, too.

What should I do if I get e-mail I don't want?

One of the hazards of having your name and e-mail address out there on the Net is that people will find it.

Don't respond directly! There are really two cases:

1. They're trying to sell you something (see, also, What are they selling?)
2. They've said something that disturbs you (see the previous section).

£££ Selling something

E-mail that offers a product, or tells you about a money-making opportunity, or describes a chain letter or other scheme, is called 'Unsolicited Commercial E-Mail' (UCE). It's more commonly known as 'spam'. Some of these things are just bad ideas; others, like chain letters, are actually illegal.

Many 'spammers' will use a fake return address; a few will use the address of someone else who complained about them. Some will give you an address to reply to in order to get off their list. Don't. In many cases, this just tells them that your address is valid and that you're reading your e-mail. They may not send you anything, but they may sell your name to somebody else.

If you really want to stop them, tell your service provider (or a parent) to contact their service provider. Often that doesn't do much good, but it's better than replying directly.

Danger signs

'Don't talk to strangers' is just as good advice on the Net as it is on the street. If you get e-mail that disturbs you, there are two possibilities, neither of them good.

1. The person sending it is using a fake or incorrect address, either to get someone else in trouble or just to hide behind it while they make you feel bad, or because they're using a machine in a public place that the previous user didn't erase their address from. (This happened to me recently, which is why I'm writing this in the first place.) In that case, replying directly will just cause the real person behind the address, if any, to think that you're accusing them of something bad. They'll be upset, if nothing else. You don't want that.

2. The person sending it is using their own address. In that case, you might be replying to a harmless pervert, or perhaps to a dangerous criminal. You don't want that, either.

In either case, have your parents or your service provider's system administration department find out who this person's service provider is, and contact their system adminis-

trator. Often it will be a user called 'postmaster'. Some of the larger service providers have a user called 'abuse' for reporting this kind of thing.

If the person's domain isn't a service provider you recognise (for example aol.com or netcom.com) it might be a private domain, and postmaster might be the person who sent you the mail in the first place.

In that case you had better contact their service provider. You can look this up using the search forms at the InterNIC http://www.internic.net

What if they want to visit me?

For kids living at home

If a friend you've met on the Net wants to visit you, or wants you to visit them, make sure that at least one of your parents gets to meet them, too. Inviting them to your house is good, or have a parent take you over to their house. Have your parents arrange things on the phone first.

If you can't arrange for a phone conversation that includes a parent on each end of the line (for example, you're trying to make all the arrangements by e-mail), or if your parents don't want to tell strangers where you live, or you just feel embarrassed about how messy your room is, you can arrange to meet in a public place (maybe at a restaurant or a local amusement park). Be sure you each have a parent along.

For young people away from home

Things are different when you're out on your own. If you're away at college, or just living in an apartment and working, be very careful about who you reveal your address, and maybe even your name and phone number, to. If you want to meet somebody you've struck up an acquaintance with on the Net, do it in a public place and bring along a friend.

- The above information is an extract from a web site which can be found on the Internet at the address www.starport.com/places/forKids/warn-kids.html

Internet usage set to slow

Information from MORI (Market & Opinion Research International Ltd.)

Until technology and transport providers offer speedier access, growth of Internet usage in Western Europe and the US will slow, according to a survey conducted by MORI International and Response Analysis Corporation USA. Most additional growth is due to come from outside the Western world.

Reasons for using/not using the Internet

While users like the breadth and depth of the information available on the Internet, they are frustrated by the 'World Wide Wait' (slow access speeds). Outside the US, telephone costs continue to be a major barrier.

The amount of information available on the Web, the speed at which you can access information and the ability to communicate with people of similar interests are considered to be key advantages of the Web.

Internet users are just as concerned about revealing personal information as they are about transactional security. Lack of time is also an issue and there is an indication that the Internet continues to be viewed as a diversion rather than a serious medium by many users and potential users.

Users consider the Net to be important in their daily lives now and that it will become even more important in the next two to three years.

Usage behaviour

Users are still exploring and learning about the Net. They are on-line fairly frequently and spend a fair amount of time on the Net during a typical session. Weekly usage ranges from six to more than nine Internet sessions while the length of a typical session ranges from a half-hour up to more than 50 minutes.

The amount of time spent on-line in a typical session seems stable. The main exceptions are the US and Greece where the highest proportion of users say their typical session has increased in length and the Netherlands where the opposite is true.

Surfing continues to account for a large proportion of time spent on-line. Users on average spend around one-third of their time on-line while the remainder of their time is spent visiting sites they have been to before.

In English speaking countries and most of Western Europe, the home is the primary venue for Internet usage. Only in Japan and Greece are users more likely to go on-line at work. Payment for the Internet is largely determined by venue.

The survey also found that the Internet is starting to replace the TV as a leisure activity. Approximately one in ten adult Internet users across all the countries surveyed claim that the Internet has almost completely or completely replaced TV watching.

Content and commerce

Consumers are more likely to regard the Internet as a reference library than a bookstore. They are more interested in using it for information purposes than to make a purchase on-line. Indeed, they are more likely to gather information and then purchase in a more traditional way.

Business-related content is still the primary driver of Internet usage while product and service information is also an important content area. Users are also very interested in timely information about local activities.

Consumers who have purchased on-line are most likely to have done so in areas which have a strong mail- and telephone-order presence. The main categories of interest are computer-related products, travel, books, event tickets and music. Banking is one of the most popular service categories. Dutch consumers are the most enthusiastic Internet purchasers while the British are among the least likely to have done so.

Technical note

MORI International and Response Analysis Corporation interviewed 2,045 Internet users in twelve countries world-wide including Australia, Canada, Finland, France, Germany, Great Britain, Greece, Italy, Japan, Netherlands, Sweden and the United States. Interviewing was conducted among current Internet users by telephone with adults aged 18+ in November 1997 – January 1998.

© MORI (Market & Opinion Research International Ltd.)

UK internet e-mail is the most developed in Europe

The UK's communication over the internet by e-mail is the most developed in Europe according to FutureTrack, the first comprehensive European study of the ownership and use of new media and the internet. It was published on 8 January 1999, by leading market research company BMRB International on behalf of its European network of agencies, Euroquest, covering 12 European countries with a representative sample of 12,000 adults.

A larger proportion of the UK's on-line population is chattering to work colleagues and friends by e-mail than any other nation in Europe. Over 50 per cent of UK internet users use e-mail to keep in contact with their friends compared with a European average of 34 per cent. Other above-average e-mailing nations are Sweden, Denmark and Finland. The lowest proportion of e-mailers are the Italians at just 18 per cent.

Scandinavians dominate internet

Overall, however, it is the Scandinavians that dominate internet usage.

More than half of the Swedish population, nearly 50 per cent of Finns and 46 per cent of Danes have used the internet. This contrasts with just under a third in the UK, the Netherlands, Eire and Austria; a quarter in France and Belgium and a fifth in Germany and Spain. Only 19 per cent of Italians have ever used the internet.

E-mail dominates in most of Europe

E-mailing friends tops work e-mail by 5 per cent in the UK with 52 per cent of internet users emailing friends compared with 47 per cent for work. Proportionately e-mailing is the top European internet activity in eight of the countries surveyed. For the Belgians and Spanish, the main use of the internet is visiting news and sports sites. In contrast, the main activity for the Italians and Dutch is researching interests and hobbies.

Visiting entertainment sites (including adult sites) is also popular, with 28 per cent of European internet users having done so. The Finnish lead the way with 50 per cent of internet users having visited entertainment sites, followed by the Austrians with 41 per cent. In the UK the figure is 28 per cent, while entertainment sites are least popular in Germany (25%).

Home vs work usage

In most countries, including the UK, more people have had experience of using the internet at work than at home. The exceptions to this pattern are Sweden, Denmark and Germany where home use is higher, and Belgium and Spain where home and work use are at similar levels. French, Irish and Austrian users are more likely to have connected at school or university than at home.

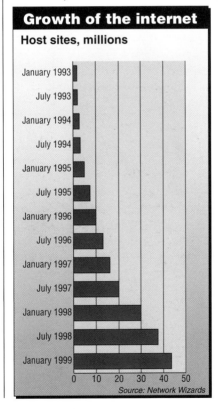

Growth of the internet

Host sites, millions

January 1993	
July 1993	
January 1994	
July 1994	
January 1995	
July 1995	
January 1996	
July 1996	
January 1997	
July 1997	
January 1998	
July 1998	
January 1999	

0   10   20   30   40   50

Source: Network Wizards

Varying frequency

Overall home users tend to connect more frequently than those using the internet elsewhere. There is also variation by country, with 45 per cent of home users in Finland connecting almost every day while 29 per cent of British and only 15 per cent of Spanish home users do so. However, although the Spanish connect less frequently, they stay on-line for longer, with an average of more than one hour each day they connect.

This compares with 50 minutes for British home users.

European e-banking is more advanced than on-line shopping

E-banking in European homes is more advanced than on-line home shopping, except in Spain, the UK and Austria. The Finns are the top home e-bankers with 44 per cent of home users participating compared with just over a fifth in Belgium, Denmark, Germany and Sweden. In the UK, it is comparatively under-developed with only 9 per cent of home users e-banking.

The most developed markets for home shopping are Sweden, Spain, Austria, Finland and the UK with between 10 and 17 per cent of users purchasing on-line. In most other European countries, on-line shopping is negligible. 'The European internet market is highly diverse.

Development is broadly-speaking more advanced in Scandinavia where the internet is becoming part of everyday life at home and as well as at work,' said Penny Sanders, BMRB International. 'In the UK we haven't reached that stage yet, but the diversity of internet use here shows that British users are among the most sophisticated in Europe.'

After hours: a smart home?

A home-owner's journal

November 28

Moved in at last. Finally, we live in the smartest house in the neighbourhood. Everything's networked. The cable TV is connected to our phone, which is connected to my PC, which is connected to the power lines, all the appliances and the security system. Everything runs off a universal remote with the friendliest interface I've ever used. Programming is a snap. I'm, like, totally wired.

November 30

Hot stuff! Programmed my VCR from the office, turned up the thermostat and switched on the lights with the car phone, remotely tweaked the oven a few degrees for my pizza. Everything nice and cosy when I arrived.

Maybe I should have the universal remote surgically attached.

December 3

Yesterday, the kitchen crashed. Freak event. As I opened the refrigerator door, the light bulb blew. Immediately, everything else electrical shut down – lights, microwave, coffee maker – everything! Carefully, I unplugged and replugged all the appliances. Nothing. Called the cable company (but not from the kitchen phone). They refer me to the utility.

The utility insists the problem was in the software. So the software company runs some remote tele-diagnostics via my house processor.

Their expert system claims it has to be the utility's fault. I don't care, I just want my kitchen back. More phone calls. More remote diagnostics.

Turns out the problem was 'unanticipated failure mode' – the network had never seen a refrigerator bulb failure while the door was open. So the fuzzy logic interpreted the burnout as a power surge and shut down the entire kitchen. But because sensor memory confirmed that there hadn't actually been a power surge, the kitchen's logic sequence was confused so it couldn't do a standard restart.

The utility guy swears this was the first time this has ever happened.

Rebooting the kitchen took over an hour.

> *Everything runs off a universal remote with the friendliest interface I've ever used. Programming is a snap. I'm, like, totally wired*

December 7

The police are not happy. Our house keeps calling them for help. We discover that whenever we play the TV or stereo above 25 decibels, it creates patterns of micro-vibrations that get amplified when they hit the window. When these vibrations mix with a gust of wind, the security sensors are actuated and the police computer concludes that someone is trying to break in.

Another glitch: whenever the basement is in self-diagnostic mode, the universal remote won't let me change the channels on my TV. That means I actually have to get up off the couch and change the channels by hand.

The software and the utility people say this flaw will be fixed in the next upgrade – SmartHouse 2.1, but it's not ready yet.

December 12

This is a nightmare. There's a virus in the house. My personal computer caught it while browsing on the public access network. I come home and the living room is a sauna, the bedroom windows are covered with ice, the refrigerator has defrosted, the washing machine has flooded the basement, the garage door is cycling up and down and the TV is stuck on the Home Shopping channel. Throughout the house,

-WE, THE HOUSE NETWORK WANT TO WATCH THE HOME SHOPPING CHANNEL, OKAY...

lights flicker like stroboscopes until they explode from the strain. Broken glass is everywhere. Of course, the security sensors detect nothing.

I look at a message slowly throbbing on my PC screen: 'Welcome to HomeWrecker!!! Now the FUN begins . . . (be it ever so humble, there's no virus like HomeWrecker . . .)' I get out of the house. Fast.

December 18

They think I've digitally disinfected the house but the place is a shambles. Pipes have burst and we're not completely sure we've got the part of the virus that attacks toilets. Nevertheless, The Exorcists (as the anti-virus SWAT members like to call themselves) are confident the worst is over. 'HomeWrecker is pretty bad,' one tells me, 'but consider yourself lucky you didn't get Poltergeist. That one is really evil.'

December 19

Apparently, our house isn't insured for viruses. 'Fires and mudslides yes,' says the claims adjuster, 'viruses, no.'

My agreement with the SmartHouse people explicitly states that all claims and warranties are null and void if any appliance or computer in my house networks in any way, shape or form with a noncertified on-line service. Everybody's very, very sorry but they can't be expected to anticipate every virus that may be created.

We call our lawyer. He laughs. He's excited.

December 21

I get a call from a SmartHouse sales rep. As a special holiday offer, we get the free opportunity to become a beta site for the company's new SmartHouse 2.1 upgrade. He says I'll be able to meet the programmers personally. 'Sure,' I tell him . . .

Selling-by-Internet stays boxed in

Internet shopping will grow swiftly over the next few years, but will nevertheless remain a tiny proportion of total retail sales by 2002, according to a report published today. Instead, direct mail will be the big growth sector, writes Roger Cowe.

The specialist researchers, Corporate Intelligence on Retailing, predict that electronic shopping will be the most exciting part of the direct mail revolution, which also includes the emergence of several major new forces, including Marks and Spencer.

But the analysis concludes that even with sixfold growth over the next five years, the Internet will still have made little impression on the huge traditional and new mail order operators.

Report author Hilary Monk says: 'We are trying to be realistic about electronic shopping. Looking at the US experience it is likely to grow quickly.

'A lot of companies will probably load their catalogues on to the Internet.

'But I don't think the big mail order companies are going to go away for some time.'

She says that last year Internet shoppers spent only £15 million, with most of the electronic business accounted for by dedicated TV channels such as QVC.

Her forecast sees these sales channels growing faster than any other area of the home shopping market, on the back of digital television and the continued penetration of multi-media personal computers.

But despite rapid growth, electronic sales are expected to reach only £720 million by 2002. That would represent only 0.35 per cent of total retail sales.

She says that consultants and information technology specialists 'with their own agendas to push' have wildly overstated the potential of Internet shopping.

Growth of 176 per cent a year would be necessary to reach the 10 per cent level predicted by some commentators.

On the contrary, CIR predicts that direct mail order catalogues will be the main driver of growth in home shopping.

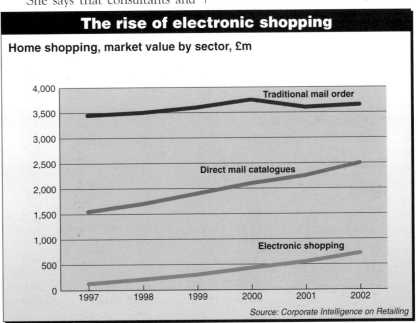

The rise of electronic shopping

Home shopping, market value by sector, £m

Source: Corporate Intelligence on Retailing

Why is Internet shopping so slow?

As the big supermarkets go on-line. Jane Furnival finds that doing the weekly shop by computer takes hours longer than slogging around on foot

Sainsbury's announced yesterday a major expansion of its Internet shopping service with the news that it will open one of the world's largest home shopping centres next year. At the moment Sainsbury's Internet shopping is limited to comparatively few stores. But from next year many thousands more customers will be able to select their orders over the Internet, and then have the goods delivered. With this in mind, Jane Furnival put the on-line services of Sainsbury's and its big rival Tesco to the test, rating categories out of three stars.

Tesco

Getting started

Called my local store. Yes, they would deliver from the Purley superstore. To register, I just contact Tesco's website, give my postcode and it tells me whether I'm in the delivery area.

Found Tesco on-line immediately by guessing address – tesco.co.uk. But had to search through mishmash of headlines like 'Win a pair of tickets to America' to find 'Internet Superstore: the UK's most exciting way to shop'. We shall see.

Once you press 'go' you get a customer number and a password. If you forget it? Don't panic, 'click here to retrieve it'. Rating: **

How to shop

You get four options: product search, shopping basket, checkout and order status. No further explanation, but I grasped it quickly. You search for your item, add it to your shopping basket, checkout, and check your delivery time and date using 'order status'. Rating: **

The tricky bit

You are given various department names on screen. Click on 'Bakery', say, and you get sub-sections: bread, savoury morning goods, sweet morning goods, cakes, seasonal puddings, instore bakery. Miss the mouth-watering smell we enjoy in the shop. All items are reduced to dry-as-dust grocers' inventory descriptions like 'ISB Scratch Doughnuts'. What's a scratch doughnut when it's at home? They don't say – and a free scratch doughnut to whoever can tell me what 'Nellie Bread' is. Rating: No stars

Counting the cost

This is very confusing. After each item's price another column listing the 'unit price'. So Tesco Value Medium Sliced White Bread costs 17p with a 'unit price' of 0.2p. Is this what it really costs the store to buy? Or will it be added to my bill? No explanation.

But you do get revealing price comparisons. Best Bacofoil costs 36p per metre; Tesco Value, 6p. Rating: *

Fruit and veg

I want some English apples. The only ones available are Cox's, listed loose at 69p 'each'. What are they, gold-coated? I change to 'red eating apples' where no country of origin is listed. Some apples are offered in pounds, others in kilos.

Nor did Tesco want to deliver any onions, peaches, exotic lettuce, peppers or organic produce. 'There are 0 products in this group' comes up continually, though I find carrots not under 'carrots' but 'core vegetables'. But of course. Silly me. Rating: No Stars

Meat

Under 'meat', a category called 'Fresh beef saleable' is puzzling. Do they sell 'unsaleable' meat, too?

I order 'freedom beef' (from free range animals?) over the virtual counter at £2.85lb for a joint. No money off there then. The trouble is, I can't find a way of ordering more than 1lb of the stuff. I couldn't order less than a kilo of sausages. Such sizeism adds pounds to your basket. Rating: *

What about wine?

Fantastic selection, listed by country and type. I ordered. Rating **

What couldn't I order?

I had looked forward to having heavier things like catfood delivered, but couldn't find them. Likewise, bottles of water or juice, tea, coffee and basic chemist stuff. So I would have to go shopping anyway. Rating: No stars

Choice

When you *do* get a choice, you get a lot of choice. 72 jams take a long time to scan. Different sizes of an item aren't listed together, so I wasted time cancelling items. Rating: *

Paying and delivery

You type in your credit card details on screen. Assurances regarding encrypted numbers appear for security. I was offered next-day delivery and a choice of times in half-hour slots. I was also asked if I minded substitutions for anything out of stock. If I did not want the thing when it arrived, they take it back and refund the price. Delivery charge is £5. Rating: *

When it arrived

Five minutes late, two nice women appeared – my Personal Shoppers. They had done the shop so knew all about it. They cheerfully climbed my stairs with all bags and helpfully pointed out frozen things first. They left before I had unpacked, but gave a shopping list and their phone number if I had any problems. Rating: ***

Results

Items I knew I'd cancelled still appeared, like paella and frozen beef and stout pie. And where was my wine? Not there. Nor any ice cream. The explanation that the freezer was on the blink was implausible, but apologies profuse and charming.

I worried that I wasn't on the spot in the supermarket to choose food with the furthest-away sell-by dates. Would the delivery people palm me off with the old food they wanted to clear from the shelves? But everything seemed OK.

There were several substitutions. Bacon ordered from the butcher's counter was replaced with a pre-packed amount and a written apology saying there was none at the counter.

I made a mistake, ordering plain cod instead of breaded, but decided it was too much hassle to call them back. I should have asked the women to wait while I unpacked the bags.

Rating: **

Bargains

No special offered flashed up on screen to tempt me. Fresh pre-packed broccoli had 50 per cent extra when it arrived; Princes' tuna chunks contained four tins for the price of three. My Tesco Clubcard points were added to my bill.

Rating: **

Next time

You can store your list on the Tesco Internet site which means you don't have to go through the long order process if you want the same next time. You get access to new products if they are on-line.

Rating: **

Total time

Fours hours and 19 minutes on-line, which BT estimates costs £5. There was also that £5 delivery charge. To shop in person would have taken me one hour with a petrol bill of £2.50.

Total rating 19 out of 45.

J Sainsbury

Getting started

Called my local store, which referred me to a nearby store in Beckenham, Kent. Yes, they deliver. But not to me. I was only two miles away but not in 'the right' postcode area. 'But,' I protested, 'your van passes my front door to deliver to Peckham, five miles on.' No chance.

Two insistent calls later, they agreed, as a special favour, to drop off to me. (Nobody said that I could have e-mailed my order and collected it ready-bagged from the store for a £3.50 charge, which I discovered by chance later.)

Unlike Tesco, you go into your store and sign up. It takes two hours to fill in forms, arrange a password, give your credit card details and receive blurb including this week's special offers.

You are then given a laser pricing gun and told to tour the store, zapping any item you might ever, conceivably, want to buy. This list, memorised by the machine, becomes your personal shopping catalogue.

Unlike Tesco, which gives you access to all the store's stock – in theory – Sainsbury only allow you to shop from your personal catalogue. At home, you can't add afterthoughts unless you go back to the store for an extra re-zap session.

Rating: No stars

How to shop

The introduction pack gives the address sainsburys.co.uk and the 'shop now' section is easily visible. But the screen is too wide to read everything, no matter how you fiddle.

Little, or nothing, of the information I had given on my forms instore got through to the system. I spent hours trying to log on. It kept me hanging on in there, by occasionally asking me to choose my delivery method – then asking me to log on again.

The Helpline advised me to use a different address – orderline.sainsburys.co.uk After another fruitless day, I called and found that nobody had entered my details.

Next day, no luck again. The Helpline said that my Internet service provider, AOL, 'interferes with the service' so shoppers on AOL have a hard time. Eventually they asked if I was working on an Apple Mac. I was. 'The system is not set up for Apple Macs. Very few customers have them.' Amazed. This had never been mentioned.

I went to the home of a friend, and using her Dell computer we logged on together. And still went round in circles. The Helpline discovered that my credit card details had never been input.

Rating: No stars

The tricky bit

Your options are: 'shopping service', 'service choice' and 'list choice'. There is no explanation. Press the help button and it just repeats the word you wanted explaining. David at the Helpline said that having made my catalogue at the shop, I would use it to draw up this week's shopping list. I needed to give it a name – Jane list – and the system remembered it. Next time, I could call it up, twiddle in a few changes and send it. A time and money-saving idea.

I was asked which store I would like to deliver: Bristol or Beckenham. Chose Beckenham. My ice cream would melt in the four hours it would take to drive to London from Bristol, but thanks for the choice.

The instruction buttons are confusing and ordering took a long time. Does 'store' mean: access to the store, or store this order? No help, as usual. A mystery button 'com' allowed a comment or request beside each item. But to specify the number of each item you wanted, you pressed the plus or minus button beside a box, which was simpler than Tesco.

A 'search' button allowed me to specify what I wanted without having to go through each food department. The list containing the word was too long for the screen.

Rating: *

Counting the cost

Simpler than Tesco. A running tariff at the top told me how much I'd spent. Found a useful button which converts weights from kilos to pounds.

Rating: **

Fruit and veg

Loads of apples, including organic. Everything I'd seen in the shop was available. Much better than Tesco.

Rating: **

Meat

No problem. Under 'com' I could specify how much money I wanted to pay for my roast joint.

Rating: **

What about wine?

Fantastic selection. Also fizzy water and children's drinks.

Rating: ***

What couldn't I order?

Bacon and tomatoes, which I had zapped in store. At one point we nearly broke the machine – 'Please close and restart your browser' flashed up after one hour, 20 minutes on-line. We finished our order on my friend's laptop Compaq.

And it took me, my pal and both our husbands to complete the order.

Rating: No stars

Choice

This didn't apply in the same way as Tesco as I had gone and zapped what I wanted beforehand.

Rating: *

Paying and delivery

I didn't notice the checkout button and had the familiar experience of being repeatedly asked to log on again, fearing my order had been lost. Eventually found the right button. They had my credit card details so I specified a delivery time – next day in two-hour timezones. Found that my address had been wrongly input.

I was offered next-day delivery and a choice of times in half-hour slots. There is a £5 per time delivery charge but the first delivery is free with a discount voucher.

Rating: No stars

When it arrived

On time, exhausted driver Tracey arrives. I felt very sorry for her: she confided that she was a sub-contractor and really needed a bag carrier but it was not economic and she was pushed hard because the service was increasingly popular. She wasn't allowed to carry bags upstairs for insurance reasons.

Rating: *

Results

The bags were beautifully packed with frozen and chilled goods labelled clearly. Tracey pointed them out so that I could put them in the freezer first.

Several substitutions were sent for me to choose from: four types of cheese – I rejected three, which were sent to the store for a refund.

I hadn't been palmed off with old food – the sell-by dates were acceptable. Both iced desserts had defrosted. Maybe the delivery came from Bristol after all.

Rating: **

Bargains

Although I ordered one pack of mince, a second pack was added because it was a half-price offer. Two hours later, Tracey reappears sweetly bearing a extra shampoo. A 'two for the price of one' offer had started that afternoon so she dropped it in. Although I had filled out my Reward Card number, no points were added.

Rating: **

Next time

You can make your order quicker by choosing the same list name again. I hop to have a faster order time. Of course I could always order by phone . . .

Rating: **

Total time

Two hours instore zapping things. Day after day of trying to work out what to do. Then four and a half hours on-line. The cutdown catalogue saved time and I knew I was ordering the right sizes.

Total rating: 18 out of 45.

Conclusion

Cyber-shopping is in its infancy and yes, it certainly does have teething troubles. Tesco should offer more choice; Sainsbury seem to be trying to do it on the cheap, but they have to train staff to keep customers properly informed.

Now I know why the woman pictured on the front of their info pack looks absolutely exhausted. Internet shopping is potentially a godsend – why did we ever get rid of delivery boys? But it will never replace bargain-hunting and the occasional outing to see new things in the shops.

© The Daily Mail
May, 1999

Firms making a Net profit from our technophobia

By Sean Poulter

Britons pay more than anyone else in Europe to connect to the Internet.

Home subscriptions to service providers cost an average of £15.40 a month in the UK compared to £8.99 in France and just £3.20 in Sweden, says a report.

Users pay their phone bill on top – normally at a local call rate for the time they are connected to the information super-highway.

The damning statistics from analysts Datamonitor suggest Internet companies are taking advantage of customers' ignorance and their fear of technology.

The high cost could slow down take-up of Internet services, which are seen as a valuable tool for children and students.

Many who are unsure about computers sign up with well-known firms such as America On Line (AOL) which have a good reputation but are expensive.

AOL has three subscription bands – £4.95 a month for up to three hours of use, £16.95 a month for unlimited access or an annual subscription of £179.40.

Datamonitor says British users are less price sensitive than other Europeans and are grateful for the extra information and services offered by large companies such as AOL and Compuserve.

> ### The high cost could slow down take-up of Internet services, which are seen as a valuable tool for children and students

The big names, however, could soon be forced to axe their charges as a raft of firms offer free connection. Dixons, which launched its Freeserve system just before Christmas, has already signed up 900,000 customers. While there is no monthly subscription, calls to the High Street giant's phone helpline can be very expensive.

Britons are already said to be overcharged for computers.

Microchip maker Intel recently complained Dixon's prices for PCs were too high. Dixons tried to rubbish the claims but the Office of Fair Trading is now investigating at the request of former Trade Secretary Peter Mandelson.

- This is the average monthly cost of connecting to the Internet across Europe: UK £15.40; Germany £14.61; Netherlands £14.02; Austria £13.77; Belgium £12.75; Switzerland £12.64; Greece £12.57; Italy £9.29; France £8.99; Spain £6.63; Finland £5.85; Norway £5.60; Denmark £5.07; Sweden £3.20.

© *The Daily Mail*
January, 1999

Trapped in the Web

Why four volunteers are trying to live by Internet alone

By David Derbyshire,
Science Correspondent

Four brave volunteers were waking up this morning at the start of their first full day in cyberspace.

The two men and two women have agreed to spend this week locked in separate small rooms with only the Internet to sustain them.

They will have to order food, drink and clothes via the Net. For company, they have e-mail – and a few million Internet voyeurs all over the world observing their progress through tiny cameras fixed in the rooms.

To protect their modesty they were each given a bathrobe at the start of the experiment yesterday.

Then they were left for the next four days, only able to communicate with the outside world through their computers linked to the Worldwide Web.

'Today everyone is talking about the Internet, but no one has put it to the test like this,' said Helen Petrie, a human and computer interaction expert from the University of Hertfordshire.

'We will observe how our volunteers cope for 100 hours with just the Internet as their support system. The results promise to be fascinating.'

The volunteers are Emma Gibson, 30, an actress from Notting Hill, West London; Robin Katz, 46, an American writer living in Hampstead, North London; Glyn Thomas 45, a freelance book editor from Hounslow, West London; and Scotsman Martin Kennedy, 67, a retired fireman from Dunstable, Bedfordshire.

They were shut into secure rooms at a central London hostel

and handed a credit card with a budget of £500 to feed themselves during the experiment, organised by Microsoft's Internet arm.

Miss Gibson said: 'I was doing a boring job after being in Australia for two years, so this is going to be the perfect opportunity for me to try and find a job.

'I am computer literate, but I don't use the Internet that much. I'll be able to e-mail my friends in Australia and find out how to emigrate there.'

Mr Kennedy is the most knowledgeable of the four about the Net.

He said: 'It seems I have been dubbed a Silver Surfer but I do find the Internet useful for keeping up with my main interests, golf and whisky.

'I don't think I will get bored, even though it's a long time. I want to use the time to research my family tree and try to get in contact with old school pals I have not seen for over 40 years.'

Robin Katz will seek out and buy music CDs, write a new CV and look for a job while Mr Thomas wants to search for toys from around the world for his niece, research a trip to Dublin, play chess, check out news sites and look at sunrises around the world.

It is now possible to buy almost anything over the Internet. Online stores will sell and deliver everything from soap and clothes to beer and takeaway meals.

The first rations to arrive yesterday were boxes of fruit, vegetables and groceries from Sainsbury's on-line service. The volunteers were allowed to order them in advance.

The e-mail chat rooms and cameras are due to be switched off between 2pm and 4pm every day during the week to give the volunteers a break. But yesterday they were so busy answering e-mails, all were still dressed in their bath robes till late in the evening.

Netlife diary – Day one Diary of a day in cyber space:

10am: The nervous volunteers are shown their rooms. They don [...] bes and watch with dismay as their clothes are taken away. The rooms are packed with TV cameras, reporters and microphones.

10.30am: The dreaded lock-in is delayed as the interviews with the world's press continue. The first pictures –from small cameras on top of each computer – begin to broadcast grainy images of the foursome across the Net.

Noon: More than 300 e-mails have come in, wishing the volunteers good luck and offering advice on where to get the best Net bargains.

2pm: The guinea pigs are taken to their rooms and the doors shut. Within a few minutes the first supplies, ordered last week, arrive at the hostel front door. Although the boxes from Kay's catalogue and Principles contain underwear, T-shirts, socks and trousers, the four are too busy replying to e-mails to dress. Shops and restaurants begin touting for their business by e-mail. Martin orders a Sony Walkman, while the others select books from on-line seller Amazon.

4pm: The live 'chat room' opens, allowing the guinea pigs to talk to the outside world. University students ask if they can use the results of the experiment in dissertations.

6pm: Still on-line. Cameras keep tabs on the four as they sit hunched over their keyboards. Every move is monitored – even when they pay a visit to their ensuite bathrooms.

7pm: The first supper shift begins. Each has 30 minutes in the kitchen to prepare food and eat before returning to their cells.

9pm: The chat rooms close, the cameras switch off and the four can sleep at last.   © *The Daily Mail May, 1999*

---

10 tips for safe Web surfing

Excerpted from *Web Psychos, Stalkers, and Pranksters* **by Michael A. Banks**

1. Maintain control of communications! Until you are certain of a new on-line acquaintance, restrict contact to e-mail, chat, and/or public postings.
2. Unless you know who you're talking to online, don't take anyone at their word as to their name, gender, occupation, location, or other information.
3. Be careful about how much and what sort of personal information you give out to those you don't know. This includes information in chats, public postings, and e-mail. Handing out your address or telephone number is the same as handing someone a key to your life.
4. If someone you've just met in a chat room is dying to talk with you via voice phone, get their number instead of giving yours.
5. Don't sign every Web site Guest Book you come across; this will only increase your load of unsolicited e-mail, as one of spammers' many sources for address lists are Guest Book entries.
6. Think before posting in public – it can come back to haunt you! Messages posted in USENET Newsgroups and certain other areas hang around for a long time, and they're searchable!
7. If you do a lot of posting in USENET Newsgroups or other public message systems, consider using a different ID for your personal e-mail.
8. To reduce or eliminate unsolicited commercial Email – and the potential for unpleasant e-mail – delete any online profiles you may have posted about yourself. Better still, don't post any public information about yourself.
9. Protect your identity and e-mail address as you browse Web pages by removing your name and e-mail address from your browser's setup or preferences section. Your browser won't tell the Web page who you are, and you can easily replace this info when you want to send mail using the browser.
10. Most online problems are preventable; staying out of trouble is easier than getting out of trouble. *Web Psychos, Stalkers, and Pranksters* can help you stay out of trouble, and deal with it if it happens!

© *1997, 1998, Michael A. Banks*

Meanwhile, back on the 'real' Net . . .

Newsgroups are lively, informative, opinionated, quarrelsome and fun. Rick Maybury invites you to join the party

Newsgroups are the heart and soul of the Internet. Think of them as the community halls of the global village, far removed from the slick big-city commercial and business interests on the World Wide Web. They're places where like-minded individuals meet on-line to discuss and swap ideas, ask and answer questions on just about any subject you care to name (and one or two you probably wouldn't).

A newsgroup is basically a public noticeboard where you can post email messages, articles or announcements for others to read and respond to. Unlike normal email and the Web, which are immediately accessible once you've signed up with an Internet Service Provider (ISP), you have to 'subscribe' to newsgroups, though it's not like a magazine or newspaper subscription and won't cost you a penny (apart from your normal on-line charges).

If you are wondering if there's a newsgroup devoted to your particular interests, the answer is undoubtedly yes. It's impossible to give a precise figure but there are well over 40,000 of them right now, with hundreds more created every day. The number of newsgroups you will have direct access to depends on your ISP. Newsgroups are stored on computers called news servers, which are part of a wider network called Usenet; apart from the problems of finite storage space, most ISPs restrict or prohibit newsgroups devoted to activities they deem antisocial or undesirable (child pornography, bomb-making, software piracy, that kind of thing).

Newsgroups may also be 'moderated' – that is, monitored for abusive or offensive messages, to keep respondents on the subject and prevent blatant advertising. In fact, there is a fairly strict code of conduct or 'netiquette' that most newsgroup users are happy to adhere to.

In order to access newsgroups you will need a program called a newsreader. The chances are you already have one on your PC, as they are integrated into most popular browsers and email programs, including Internet Explorer, Netscape and those supplied by AOL and CompuServe. Separate newsreader software programs are also available, one of the most popular being a shareware program called Free Agent, which can be downloaded from www.forteinc.com.

The first task is to set up your newsreader. You will need a couple of items of information, namely your email address and the domain name of your ISP's news server. You should find this included in the sign-up information, or you can get it from the ISP's helpline – it will usually be something like 'news.freebienet.co.uk'.

In Outlook Express, set-up begins when you click the Read News icon on the opening page. Just follow the instructions and when it has finished you will be asked if you want to download the list of newsgroups on the ISP's news server. This can take several minutes, depending on the speed of your connection and time of day. You should only have to do this once, since most newsreaders will automatically update the list when you are on-line.

The newsreader will log off and present you with a list of several thousand newsgroups. Don't bother searching through them all; it will take forever. Your newsreader has a search facility that looks for groups containing a keyword. You can then select those that interest you by clicking on the subscribe button. Incidentally, you might be wondering what all the prefixes mean. Any newsgroup beginning with 'comp' means it is computer-related, 'misc' is miscellaneous, 'rec' is short for recreational subjects, 'sci' is used for science-related topics, 'soc' covers social issues, and so on.

By far the largest collection of newsgroups begin with 'alt' for alternative. The alt groups are a kind of fringe operation, existing outside the official Usenet system but that doesn't mean they're any less interesting or useful, though this tends to be where the more dubious newsgroups congregate.

Once you have chosen the groups you wish to subscribe to, you will have to go back on-line, and the newsreader will download all of the 'headers' in your selected groups. Headers are topics or subject headings (by default OE loads 300 headers, but you can change that by going to Options on the Tools menu and selecting the Read tab). Depending on the newsgroup, you may see anything from a dozen to several hundred postings. Those marked with a plus sign indicate the message is part of a 'thread' – in effect, a running conversation.

You can read any message simply by clicking on the header. However, all the time you are on-line you are clocking up the phone bill. The alternative is to download selected messages – or the whole newsgroup, if there are not too many of them – and read them at your leisure, off-line. In Outlook Express, the option to mark and download messages can be found on the Tools menu.

You will probably find that some messages or articles no longer exist, or that you receive an error message. Don't worry – it's not a fault on your PC: messages are routinely deleted to make way for new ones and on really busy newsgroups postings may be shown only for a couple of days.

After reading a few messages you might well decide that you have something to contribute or a question to ask, but it is a good idea to read all of the postings in your chosen group. It's worth monitoring a newly subscribed newsgroup for a while to get a feel of how it works, pick up the jargon and maybe get to know the people using it. Many newsgroups include a FAQ (frequently asked questions) file about the group, and you should read it.

• First published in *The Daily Telegraph*, April, 1998. © *Rick Maybury*

Issues for families

Information from the Parents Information Network

The Internet is a very valuable resource from which everyone can benefit. It is also fascinating, exciting and great fun but, like any powerful tool, it can be misused.

• For most people, the advantages of having access to the Internet easily outweigh the disadvantages, but there is understandable concern about some material on the Internet which is inappropriate for children and young people. Certainly pornography and extremist material are available on the Web but are harder to stumble across than media reports may have led you to believe.

• Many families use 'filter software' such as CyberPatrol or NetNanny to block specified types of pictures, words or newsgroups and chatlines. The Recreational Software Advisory Council also rates Web site content and some browsers can be programmed to reject sites with 'adults only' ratings. Whilst none of these provide guaranteed safeguards, they can offer some level of control.

• There have also been cases of paedophiles using the Internet to approach children but, if children follow certain commonsense rules, they are highly unlikely to be approached in this way.

• However, no method of protection is fail-safe and parents and teachers still need to guide their children's Internet usage and be aware of what they are doing on the Net. There are some guidelines for on-line safety below.

Internet dos and don'ts

It is good to have discussed and agreed some commonsense points with your children about appropriate usage:

Do keep the computer in a family area where you can keep an eye on how it's being used. It is not a good idea to have it in a child's bedroom.

Do get involved and take an interest in how the computer is being used. Try to learn some of the basics, either from your children or by going on a starter course, or both.

Do encourage your children to tell you or another adult if they come across people, text or images which upset them.

Do report anything you think is illegal or offensive to the Internet Watch Foundation by calling 01223 236077 or www.internetwatch.org.uk/

Do complain to your service provider or, in the case of potentially illegal material, the police, if you come across offensive on-line content.

Do remember that there are other places you can find information such as local libraries, where you can talk to someone and be helped to find what you're looking for.

Do make it clear to your children that they must never meet someone they've struck up an on-line friendship with unless they discuss it with you first and are accompanied by an adult.

Don't under any circumstances give personal information such as where you live, your phone number or school name to people contacted on-line. Be wary even when you think you know them.

Don't allow children ever to give credit card details or their password to anyone.

Don't respond to someone who's pestering you on-line. Ignore them, go somewhere else on the Web or log off altogether.

Don't respond to suggestive or rude messages.

Access times and awareness of costs

Do take advantage of cheap phone rates in the evening and at weekends, although these are also the times when the Internet is likely to be particularly busy, which can slow things down.

Do read your emails and write your replies while you are not connected to the Internet, actually making the connection only to send and receive mail so that you keep costs to a minimum.

Don't get lost browsing through the mass of information available. Be aware of time and know when it's best to cut your losses!

• The above information is from the Parents Information Network, PO Box 16394, London, SE1 3ZP. Tel: 0171 357 9078. Fax: 0171 357 9077. Web site: www.pin-parents.com
© *Parents Information Network (PIN)*

Additional Resources

Back	Forward	Home	Reload	Images	Open	Print	Find	Stop

| Live Home Page | Search | Computer | Support | System |

The Internet has been likened to shopping in a supermarket without aisles. The press of a button on a Web browser can bring up thousands of sites but working your way through them to find what you want can involve long and frustrating on-line searches. And unfortunately many sites contain inaccurate, misleading or heavily biased information. Our researchers have therefore undertaken an extensive analysis to bring you a selection of quality Web site addresses.

*****

Centre for On-Line Addiction

www.netaddiction.com

The Centre for On-Line Addiction, the world's first consultation firm, training institute, and treatment centre for Internet addiction, was founded in 1995. Their staff provides a range of professional services including on-site consultation, seminars, and personalised executive coaching that focus on behavioural healthcare solutions for cyber-wellness. Web site articles include the following: What is Internet addiction (IA)? What is cybersexual addiction? Do you spend too much time on-line? What are the risk factors involved with IA? What makes the Internet so addictive? How spouses deal with cyberaffairs. Kids and computers – addiction and media violence. How to stop Internet misuse at college. Dealing with Internet misuse and the workplace. How do you treat Internet addiction? Men, women, and the Internet: Gender differences. Compulsive on-line gambling, shopping, and trading.

CIAC

http://ciac.llnl.gov/ciac/CIACHoaxes.html

The Internet is constantly being flooded with information about computer viruses and Trojans. However, interspersed among real virus notices are computer virus hoaxes. While these hoaxes do not infect systems, they are still time-consuming and costly to handle. The CIAC Web site describes a number of the hoax warnings that are found on the Internet today. Check out their information on chain letters too.

Cyberangels

www.cyberangels.org

A huge Internet safety and education program. They have been doing this since 1995. Some of the interesting sections include: Families on-line, Protecting yourself on-line, Need help and support?, Stuff for kids and teens, Internet law and policy, A parent's guide to the Internet, Sophia's safe surfing club, Kids' safety quiz, Cyber kids news and Super safe kid.

NCH Action for Children

www.nchafc.org.uk

NCH's Web site includes a number of interesting articles about the Internet including: A Parents' Guide to the Internet; Help to make the Net a safer place; and House Rules. There is also a PDF of the full booklet Children on the Internet – Opportunities and Hazards [272K].

Internet Watch Foundation (IWF)

www.internetwatch.org.uk

The Internet Watch Foundation (IWF) was launched in 1996 to address the problem of illegal material on the Internet, with particular reference to child pornography. Broadly IWF aims to enhance the enormous potential of the Internet to inform, educate, entertain and conduct business by: hindering the use of the Internet to transmit illegal material, particularly child pornography; encouraging the classification of legal material on the Net in order to enable users to customise the nature of their experience of the Net to their own requirements.

familyguidebook.com

www.familyguidebook.com/index.html

This site has been designed to be the one stop for parents, teachers, educators, librarians, law enforcement, journalists, child advocacy groups, kids, teens and college students who want to enjoy cyberspace, safely . . . They warn you about the dangers and risks on-line, help you get to know each other and share the wonders of the Internet. A useful site.

National Center for Missing & Exploited Children (NCMEC)

www.ncmec.org

Has an Internet safety quiz for young people. Try it.

Notes, Advice and Warnings for Kids on the Web

http://places.to/places/forKids/warn-kids.html

Has notes, advice and warnings for children and parents tagged to its suggested links and it also has good summaries of the actual content to be found on its linked sites

Parents Information Network (PIN)

www.pin-parents.com

PIN is an independent organisation set up to help parents become more informed, confident users of computers, software and the Internet. PIN advises on how computers support the learning process – how they are used in schools and how they can support learning at home and in the wider community – by children and the whole family. PIN is currently developing a brand new, much more interactive Web site as part of its move to charitable status. In the meantime the following items on their present site are worth a look: Safe surfing for the family, Guidance for families, Starter packs, Buying a computer and printer, buying educational software, Software recommendations: PIN's independent recommendations of educational software.

KidSafe Explorer

www.arlington.com.au

The demand for family-friendly browsers is only likely to grow and KidSafe Explorer is hoping to tap into that demand. From Australia's Arlington Technology, the browser will only visit a set of sites pre-set by parents or teachers and won't even follow links from those sites to the greater Web. Lists compiled for KidSafe can also be shared, opening the way for teachers to compile one list and share it among a whole class. There is a 30-day trial version available, the full version costs US $25 for an individual, $125 for a school licence and $625 for a world-wide licence.

Recreational Software Advisory Council

www.rsac.org/homepage.asp

Provide a simple, yet effective rating system for Web sites which both protects children and protects the rights of free speech of everyone who publishes on the World Wide Web. They have also designed a system based on the tried and tested content advisory system used for computer games and one which could be simply understood and set by parents at either the browser level (e.g. Microsoft's Internet Explorer) or blocking devices (e.g. CyberPatrol).

SafeKids.Com

www.safekids.com

You'll find tips, advice and suggestions to make your family's on-line experience fun and productive.

SafeTeens.Com

www.safeteens.com

A public awareness campaign about general safety for teenagers on the Internet.

The Police Notebook

www.ou.edu/oupd

A wealth of information on Internet safety. Articles include the following: Tips & tools for parents – keeping kids safe on-line (an excellent guide to Internet safety for parents from The Children's Partnership), Is your child 'wired' yet? (a list of Internet safety resources for parents), Notes, advice, and warnings for parents and kids (advice for parents to read through with their kids to promote family discussion about DOs and DON'Ts about the Internet), Kid safety on the Internet (a broad guide on all types of safety issues written for kids), Romance on the Internet (advice for adults about meeting people and giving out personal information on the internet), Inmates seeking online 'cybermates' (an article regarding prison inmates seeking partners on the Internet), Your money and the Internet (advice for adults about shopping and transmitting financial information on the internet), On-line ordering – risky business? (how safe is it to shop on-line, really? This article may help), Know your online shopping rights (what are your legal rights when you're buying on-line?) Computer virus hoaxes (information about identifying and dealing with both real and fake computer 'virus alerts'), E-mail chain letters (information on dealing with e-mail 'chain letters' and hoaxes), Dealing with spam (information on dealing with e-mail 'spam').

INDEX

ACKNOWLEDGEMENTS

The publisher is grateful for permission to reproduce the following material.

While every care has been taken to trace and acknowledge copyright, the publisher tenders its apology for any accidental infringement or where copyright has proved untraceable. The publisher would be pleased to come to a suitable arrangement in any such case with the rightful owner.

Chapter One: The Internet in Schools

Top marks: the web shows the way, © Debbie Davies, March 1999, *Getting on the Net*, © BBC Online, *Computers can do a better job than teachers, says Blair aide*, © The Daily Mail, *You can't beat chalk and talk*, © Telegraph Group Limited, London 1999, *A computer is only as good as its master*, © Rachelle Thackray, March 1999, *Computers with no common sense*, © Michio Kaku, March 1999, *New face of homework*, © Telegraph Group Limited, London 1998, *Who's online*, © 1997 World Fact Book, Central Intelligence Agency (CIA), *Parents get on-line for class check*, © The Daily Mail, May 1999, *Pupils in peril on the Internet*, © The Daily Mail, April 1998, *World-wide use*, © 1997 World Fact Book, Central Intelligence Agency (CIA), *Community action to plug growing gap*, © The Guardian, March 1999, *Internet safety quiz for kids*, © The National Center for Missing & Exploited Children, *Safety on the internet*, © 1998 The Children's Partnership, *Don't jump too soon*, © Jim McClellan, January 1999, *Which of the following does you child use a PC for?*, © The British and Technology, Motorola/MORI.

Chapter Two: The Internet in the Home

Families switch off television to surf the Internet, © Telegraph Group Limited, London 1998, *Access at home*, © iriS/MORI (Market & Opinion Research International Ltd.), *What is Internet addiction?*, © Illinois Institute for Addiction Recovery (IIAR)/ Proctor Hospital, 1998, *The Internet addiction test*, © The Center for On-Line Addiction, *The Which? Online Annual Internet Survey*, © Which? Online, *Spam*, © 1997, University of Oklahoma, *Chain letters*, © 1997, University of Oklahoma, *How to shake off that virus*, © Telegraph Group Limited, London 1999, *Teen safety on the information highway*, © The National Center for Missing & Exploited Children, *Notes, advice and warnings*, © 1995-98 by Stephen Savitzky, *Internet usage set to slow*, © MORI (Market & Opinion Research International Ltd.), *UK internet e-mail is most developed in Europe*, *Growth of the internet*, © Network Wizards, *After hours: a smart home?*, 1996-1998 Techmall, *Selling-by-Internet stays boxed in*, © The Guardian, August 1998, *The rise of electronic shopping*, © Corporate Intelligence on Retailing, *Why is Internet shopping so slow?*, © The Daily Mail, May 1999, *Firms making a Net profit from our technophobia*, © The Daily Mail, January 1999, *Trapped in the Web*, © The Daily Mail, May 1999, *10 tips for safe Web surfing*, © 1997-1998, Michael A. Banks, *Meanwhile, back on the 'real' Net . . .*, © Rick Maybury, April 1998, *Issues for families*, © Parents Information Network.

Photographs and illustrations:

Pages 1, 6, 10, 12, 17, 23, 27, 30, 31, 32,39: Simon Kneebone, pages 4, 14, 19, 22, 24, 36: Pumpkin House.

Craig Donnellan
Cambridge
September, 1999

The Work Revolution

ISSUES
(formerly Issues for the Nineties)

Volume 25

Editor

Craig Donnellan

Independence
Educational Publishers
Cambridge

First published by Independence
PO Box 295
Cambridge CB1 3XP
England

© Craig Donnellan 1999

British Library Cataloguing in Publication Data
The Work Revolution – (Issues Series)
I. Donnellan, Craig II. Series
331.2'5

ISBN 1 86168 093 7

Printed in Great Britain
The Burlington Press
Cambridge

Typeset by
Claire Boyd

Cover
The illustration on the front cover is by
Pumpkin House.